WHEN EVANGELICALS SNEEZE

"In *When Evangelicals Sneeze,* Michael Cooper sounds a clear and chilling alarm for the evangelical church in America. Dr. Cooper calls for swift and serious action to reclaim the theological and historical foundations of our evangelical churches from what he calls 'Trumpgelicalism,' a new religious movement based in a conflation of a political agenda and religious practices. This timely book prompts us to deep self-reflection and asks us to return to our first love- the glory of God alone. Well done!"

Kathy Richards Bhatia, MDiv, BCC
MENA Regional Director
She is Safe

"Dr. Cooper's latest book is a valuable contribution to the important conversations going on at present about the state of American (White) evangelicalism. Those less familiar with the origins and history of evangelicalism will appreciate his knowledgeable summary and those less familiar with serious issues confronting this branch of Christianity in 2020 will appreciate how well he describes the situation and identifies what is at stake for American evangelism.

"Perhaps the most important and distinctive contributions, however, are his analysis of evangelicalism's alliance with the political right – what he calls Trumpgelicals – using the rubric of characteristics of new religious movements (NRMs), a field of study in which he has specialized, and his prescriptions for evangelicalism to reclaim its true God-given identity and calling. Highly recommended."

William J. Moulder
Professor of Biblical Studies
Trinity International University

"Michael has done a masterful job of crafting a study of the state of evangelicalism and charting of a way forward. He paints a tragic but accurate picture of the unfortunate coalescing of the church and politics that does damage to the Church's global and local witness. Coining and unpacking "Trumpgelicals" is a valuable task as he hopes to re-define or reclaim evangelicalism. Faithful Jesus followers who seek to also be civic minded would be undoubtedly challenged and blessed by this timely book."

Arman Sheffey
Executive Director
Unshackled Network

"Michael Cooper has effectively plotted the location of American evangelicalism on a map that seems to morph with every changing social, religious, and political wind. Not always pretty, certainly painful, but absolutely necessary, Michael offers a thoughtful critique of the current state of evangelicalism that needs to be heard. In these pages, he has shed light on an evangelical cognitive dissonance that threatens both evangelical witness within the United States, and both individual and congregational faithfulness to Jesus and the mission He left for His Church. With much research and biblical support, this work offers a way forward, a call to go back to Scripture, learn from the Church's history, and faithfully apply our individual and corporate identity in Christ to our current context. With much hope, I see Michael as giving American evangelicals the opportunity to reclaim our true identity in Christ over the against the sour pottage it has become."

David Feiser
Pastor
Round Hill Evangelical Presbyterian Church
Crossroads, PA

In *When Evangelicals Sneeze*, Michael Cooper ably exposes the major weakness of the American evangelical church: it's marriage to political parties, and, especially, Donald Trump. This marriage prevents evangelicals from fully engaging in its mission in this world: to proclaim the Gospel message, to defend the faith, and to work toward making the world a more just place. Fortunately for us, Cooper provides a path forward, returning to our first-century roots to reclaim who we are as evangelical Christ-followers and re-engage the world for the sake of God's glory and Christ's Gospel. It also provided me, in my role as a pastor shepherding and evangelical church, with hope and clarity for how to best live into my calling and help my congregation be more faithful to our mission.

Steve Hoffman
Senior Pastor
Covenant Community Church
Fairfield, OH

WHEN EVANGELICALS SNEEZE

CURING THE AMERICAN CHURCH FROM THE PLAGUE OF IDENTITY LOSS

EPHESIOLOGY PRESS

When Evangelicals Sneeze: Curing the American Church from the Plague of Identity Loss

© 2020 Michael T. Cooper

First published in 2020 by EPHESIOLOGY PRESS (http://ephesiology.com)

eBook Edition, ASIN: B08CDX48NN

Paperback Edition, ISBN: 9798664568646

All Scripture quotations, unless otherwise noted, are taken from the Holy Bible, English Standard Version. Copyright 2001 by Crossway, a publishing ministry of Good News Publishers. Used by permission. All rights reserved.

Cover photo: Bermix Studio

EPIGRAPH

"When France sneezes, the rest of Europe catches a cold."

Klemens von Metternich

A dangerous virus spreads through the American church infecting nearly 100 million church goers. What can you do to mitigate the looming catastrophe of the American evangelical plague?

"Though they know God's righteous decree that those who practice such things deserve to die, they not only do them but give approval to those who practice them. Therefore you have no excuse, O man, every one of you who judges. For in passing judgment on another you condemn yourself, because you, the judge, practice the very same things." (Romans 1:32-2:1)

DEDICATION

To my evangelical brothers and sisters around the world in hopes that this meager attempt to make sense out of evangelicalism will help you understand how the issues of race, plagues, and politics resulted in the loss of an American evangelical identity.

And to my mother who introduced me to the world of politics when I was in grade school. I have vivid memories of her working on the campaigns of West Virginia Senator Robert Byrd and West Virginia House Delegate Stephen C. Bird.

ACKNOWLEDGEMENTS

A book is never written in isolation from outside influence and this one is no different. There are many who have influenced me and most of them are enumerated in the reference list. However, I would be remiss if I did not mention a few specific people.

My co-hosts on the Ephesiology Podcast, Andrew Johnson and Matt Till, are always an encouragement as we muddle through understanding the most significant movement in the New Testament, the church in Ephesus. These are guys who respectfully allow me to have a voice unlike a few social media detractors who see no value in an old white male or take what he says as the application of a liberal hermeneutic. Andrew and Matt both model graciousness and bring a smile to my face when we are together.

My family continues to inspire me perhaps now more than ever. How I long for them to live among evangelicals who believe in Jesus, who behave with compassion, and who belong together in a community where He is proclaimed to all the nations.

"To the King of the ages, immortal, invisible, the only God, be honor and glory forever and ever. Amen." (1 Timothy 1:17)

TABLE OF CONTENT

LIST OF TABLES, GRAPHS, DIAGRAMS

FOREWORD

The theme of lost identity has been a popular one in entertainment, explored in a number of films and television programs. While this may make for interesting amusement in the fictional productions of Hollywood, it becomes troubling when the phenomenon moves from the movie theater and television screen to the real world of religion and politics. This is what has taken place with American evangelicalism: a loss, confusion or change of identity, particularly through its connections to politics from the late 1970s into the present.

This identity loss is illustrated by the different moral positions evangelicals took in two presidential impeachments. In 1993, President Bill Clinton was under assault and fighting for his political life when his sexual activities with an intern in the White House became public knowledge. Republicans and evangelicals alike assailed Clinton, not only because of perjury related to attempts to deny the activities, but also because of the moral failings related to Clinton's actions. Evangelicals supported the impeachment of Clinton because, as many said, "Character counts." As evangelicals viewed it, Clinton's sexual immorality made him unfit to continue in the presidency. The Democrats considered things very differently. For them, what took place between the president and the intern was a private matter between two consenting adults, which had no bearing on Clinton's fitness to hold the office.

This moral narrative switched dramatically with the candidacy of Donald Trump for president in 2016. Evangelicals rallied behind Trump despite numerous moral failings that included two divorces, marital infidelities that also involved paying a porn star and having her sign a non-disclosure agreement to cover up an affair, accusations of sexual misconduct, dishonesty, and problematic rhetoric and stances toward immigrants and refugees. Astonishingly, despite having a moral record that violated evangelical concerns for the sanctity of marriage, and honesty, evangelicals supported Trump in large numbers. As Cooper notes in chapter two, 81 percent of White evangelicals voted for Trump according to Pew Research Center. In fact, as of the time of the writing of this Foreword, the Public Religion Research Institute reports that 62 percent continue to approve.

Democrats, however, having given Clinton a pass for sexual indiscretions, stood firmly in opposition to Trump on moral issues, with the House Judiciary Committee holding hearings on the porn star controversy. Over the course of 23 years, the political parties switched their moral narratives, as did evangelicals, supporting a president who never would have never been viable in years past.

How should we understand the evangelical embrace of moral positions that in previous years would have put a candidate out of bounds for electoral consideration? In order to answer this question we must first acknowledge the complexity and multifaceted nature of the phenomenon. It resists simple analysis, but it seems clear that evangelical identities changed, and the morphing process took place, because evangelicals are shaping their identities by swimming in American cultural shallows rather than through dives in the deep waters of historical and biblical reflection, something *When Evangelicals Sneeze* attempts.

Two elements of American culture seem especially significant in contributing to evangelical identity loss. The first is a commitment to Christian nationalism. In trying to come to grips with why so many White evangelicals supported Trump, journalists, as well as social and political scientists have argued for a variety of explanatory factors including economic, misogynistic, racist, Islamophobic, and xenophobic. While each of these have surfaced during Trump's time in office, social psychological research indicates that even when controlling for these elements, an ideological commitment to Christian nationalism is the better predictor of evangelical support for Trump.

Christian nationalism can be defined as the conflation of religious and national identities, one which according to Whitehead, Perry and Baker (2018), "draws its roots from 'Old Testament' parallels between America and Israel, who was commanded to maintain cultural and blood purity, often through war, conquest, and separatism." In essence, through an embrace of Christian nationalism, evangelicals were and are willing to support a president who they believe can maintain a Judeo-Christian country. This can create a perspective of "us vs. them," the redeemed in God's chosen and blessed nation vs. the theologically condemned outsiders who threatens contamination and deviation from the divine national script. The embrace of

Christian nationalism by many evangelicals is one piece of the puzzle in understanding identity loss and confusion.

Another significant cultural element contributing to this process are the conspiracy theories of the internet-based QAnon. In an extensive must-read article, particularly for Christian leaders, LaFrance (June 2020) tells the story of this online community originating through an anonymous individual, "Q," who claimed to work at the highest levels of the federal government. "Q" has posted a series of claims on internet forums about things involving the "deep state," and conspiracies involving liberal Democratic figures like Hillary Clinton and George Soros, as well as allegations that the COVID-19 virus is a hoax created by the government in order to control the population. QAnon ideas have been widely embraced by many Trump supporters, especially evangelicals, where they have been combined with prophetic "end-times" scenarios found in Fundamentalist Dispensationalism. The result is an increasing fear and paranoia among evangelicals, a gross lack of discernment and wisdom, that results not only in a diminished ability to engage in critical thinking, but also a further compromise of evangelical identity.

This loss of evangelical identity, forged in connection with questionable aspect of American culture, has serious ramifications, not the least of which is a loss of credibility in the broader culture. According to the Barna Research Group, U.S. adults perceive evangelicals through the lens of politics rather than theology or faith-inspired actions of compassion and justice. As a result, only 3 out of

10 Americans have a "positive" perception of evangelicals, with 15 percent holding "somewhat negative" and 10 percent "very negative" perceptions.

With the fundamentalist-evangelical split in the 1940s, one of the ways evangelicals distinguished themselves was by the desire to engage the culture around them, and in constructive ways. If this is to remain a part of evangelical identity for the future, critical self-reflection is in order. Our dramatic turnaround in our moral platform, and our frequent embrace of political and theological conspiracies have contributed to an increasing lack of credibility by the broader culture. It may take us decades to recover.

The current state of affairs sets the stage for evangelicals to reflect anew on who they are, and who they might become. In this volume, Michael Cooper helps readers as they explore the issues related to how evangelicals lost their identity that was forged in the past, and how they might regain a more historic and biblical sense of it. Whether you are trying to understand your evangelical faith identity, or shape it into something new, this book serves as an important guide in your journey.

John W. Morehead

Director

Evangelical Chapter of the Foundation for Religious Diplomacy

WHEN EVANGELICALS SNEEZE

Western society is no longer looked upon as the sanctuary of Christianity. Instead, it is clear that the focus of Christianity has shifted from the northern hemisphere to the southern. However, the American evangelical voice seems to still resonate across the globe. In March 2020, I was invited to make a presentation to the faculty at Mission India Theological Seminary in Nagpur, Maharashtra. The topic: "What in the world is going on?" I opened the presentation with a version of a quote from Klemens von Metternich, a 19th century diplomat who reportedly quipped, "When France sneezes, the rest of Europe catches a cold."

It was just before the exponential growth of COVID-19 cases and I had no idea about the impact of the virus in the United States. My point with the faculty was theological if not ecclesiological, "When the American church sneezes, the world catches a cold." That is, what happens in the church in America will eventually happen around the world. We most definitely saw this 30 years ago, after the fall of communism in Romania. New churches wanted to be like Rick Warren's Saddleback Church or Bill Hybels' Willowcreek Community Church.

The spread of America's influence, some might say disease, on churches around the world does not go unnoticed. The question we ought to wrestle with is simply, "Is this a good thing?" Sometimes it most definitely is. But at other times, we are immune to what we export. So, I wanted to help the faculty with a better understanding of what they might expect coming from the United States in the near future. *When Evangelicals Sneeze* comes out of my attempt to help our brothers and sisters around the world make sense out of what goes on in the American church.

I also hope this book will help Americans. As a nation divided over a pandemic, racial tensions, and political candidates, we are on the verge of collapse. In some ways, it is to be expected. If we are students of history, we would recognize the similarities of the current situation in the United States with that of the Roman Empire. It was during times of crisis – plagues, civil unrest, poverty – that outside forces took advantage of a vulnerable empire and it ultimately crumbled. It didn't happen overnight. It took decades if not centuries. But it did happen.

Most interestingly, it was in the midst of this tumultuous Roman Empire that Christianity flourished. That is not happening in the United States. In fact, Christianity in general and evangelicalism specifically stands in severe trouble. A compound for the perfect plague has formed around the US religious landscape: 1) the irrelevance of the legacy church (Packard 2015, Barna 2020); 2) the heretical beliefs of a majority of evangelicals (State of Theology, 2018); 3) distrust of pastors (Brenan, 2017). If things do not change, the exponential decline of the legacy church will result in a church-less America.

WHERE WE'RE HEADING

There are three areas of ministry in the New Testament church and they are not the parking lot attendants, nursery workers, or ushers. Over the last 30 years, I've attempted to focus on each of these although not simultaneously nor with a biblical conviction that there are only three areas until recently. During my research on a New Testament movement that started in Ephesus in 51 AD, I began to see these three areas as distinct manifestations of Jesus's focus: the Greatest Commandment (love the one true God, Matt 22:37-38), the Great Compassion (care for the marginalized and exploited, Matt 25:31-40), and the Great Commission (make disciples, Matt 28:18-20). In the vernacular, they are simply apologetics, social justice, and the declaration of God's glory to the nations (i.e. disciple making).

In *Ephesiology: The Study of the Ephesian Movement*, I lay out what I believe to be the primary focus of the church. Namely, the Great Commission, the church's first love. That first love accentuates the missiologically theocentric passion to join with God in His mission to unite all things in Christ through the proclamation of the gospel to every ethnic group. This "first love" compelled the young movement in Ephesus to continue toward the completion of God's mission as prophesied in Revelation,

> *After this I looked, and behold, a great multitude that no one could number, from every nation, from all tribes and people and languages, standing before the throne and before the Lamb, clothed in White robes, with palm branches in their hands. (Rev 7:9)*

In February 2021, a new volume on social justice will be released, *Social Injustice: An Evangelical Voice in Tumultuous Times*, a follow up to a book Bill Moulder and I edited in 2011 with a similar title, *Social Injustice: What Evangelicals Need to Know About the World*. Kathy Richards Bhatia and I are editing the 10-year anniversary edition that is turning into a remarkable resource with contributions by evangelicals from around the world. Its focus provides a solid evangelical rationale for our involvement in social justice, i.e. the Great Compassion.

The volume you currently possess focuses on the defense of the evangelical faith, an apologetic if you will. The events over the past four years have raised new concerns about the identity of evangelicalism, at least among some. Today, if you were to say you were evangelical, people would label you as a Trump supporting, gun-carrying, politically conservative individual whose goal centers on legislating morality based on the conviction that America is a Christian nation. So, who has the right to define the term "evangelical?" If given to the media, evangelical would be synonymous with the description above. If left to the general public, no doubt influenced by the media, the same. I'm not saying that evangelicalism suffers from an undeserved prejudice or even bias. Apparently for the media and general public to arrive at such a description, evangelicals must also be complicit in forming it. Yet, this evangelicalism remains foreign to many around the world.

We are at a pivotal point in the history of Christianity in the United States. Its future can literally have global ramifications. With more than 65 million US adults leaving the church – a population greater than all of Albania, Jordan, Syria, Israel, and Greece combined – resources for the American church, both financial and human, could potentially become scarce. The recent Barna study, when generalized to the US adult population, suggests there could be another 43 million practicing Christians who no longer attend church on-line or in person since the outbreak of COVID-19. The evangelical church is in a precarious position as non-profit CFOs predict a dramatic decline in giving to churches and missions organizations (Kuntz and Holcombe, 2020).

Perhaps this is a manic form of a pseudo-Augustinian predestination for the American church. Perhaps the American church is intended to decline and eventually fade away. Perhaps God is indeed finished with the American church. Perhaps there is no cure for the plague we face. However, I'd like to hope that we, the church in America, might awaken to Augustine's contemporary, a fourth century North African neo-platonic philosopher by the name of Marius

Victorinus. His call abides still today, "The gospel is to be carried abroad. It is to be preached among the nations. Wherever, then, it is preached, it must be heard. But so that all may hear, one must use one's feet to travel. And so do we travel with haste and urgency" (*Commentary on the Letter to the Ephesians* 2.6.15). That gospel, the good news about Jesus Christ, the *euangelion*, defines evangelicalism. If we are not on this mission then we do not deserve to bear that moniker.

Some say we need to pray for a revival in America. Absolutely. But God has given the followers of His Son the fantastic responsibility to join with Him in His relentlessly passionate pursuit of relationships with all people. Yes, pray for revival. And also join with God on His mission. It should be the one thing that unites us as evangelicals.

WHAT TO EXPECT

In the next 12 chapters, I'm going to attempt to define evangelicalism. An aspect of defining evangelicalism should delineate it from what it is not. Since 2016, a New American Religion (NAR) threatens to usurp evangelicalism, a religious and political virus I've come to call Trumpgelicalism. I realize that once I use the term "Trumpgelical" that I have violated one of my own principles. Namely, I believe adherents of a belief or ideology have the right to define their identity, including their name. So, for example, Islam should have the right to define itself just as evangelicalism should have the right to define itself. That being said, I am honestly at a loss in how to distinguish that religiously aligned, politically conservative group of individuals who call themselves evangelical and continue their unfettered support for Donald J. Trump. This group does not represent the evangelicalism I know, nor does it represent the evangelicalism I've seen around the world, and it certainly doesn't represent the historic understanding of evangelicalism.

What I am most interested in doing in this book is clearly defining evangelicalism by its historic identity, but more importantly by its identity in a counter-intuitive reformation. This reformation goes against the grain of most things the American evangelical church has held dear: attractional services, volunteerism, Sunday monologues. It takes a first century authority marked by a core set of beliefs, a common set of behaviors, and a community of belonging so distinct from any other religious expression that its very presence in a society draws people's attention to Jesus Christ, not to a political platform.

So, chapter 1 will begin with a preliminary definition of evangelicalism. Chapter 2 will attempt a description of Trumpgelicalism and distinguish it from evangelicalism. Chapter 3 looks at the apolitical character of Jesus Christ. His obvious ambivalence to political parties should not be mistaken for a disinterest in disrupting social norms and He provides a lesson as much for evangelical Republicans as for evangelical Democrats. Chapter 4 challenges us to be courageous leaders who are willingly and constructively self-critical, especially in a time of racial and political tensions. Chapter 5 asks the question of whether or not we might be seeing the death of evangelicalism as we once knew it while chapter 6 asks if God might be finished with the

American church. Chapter 7 suggests that there still might be a cure for evangelicalism, but it is going to take some work if not also God's healing hand. Then, chapters 8, 9, and 10 look at three theologians who might help us define evangelicalism by considering church history. Chapter 11 will evaluate these attempts. Finally, chapter 12 focuses on a definition of a counter-intuitive reformation of evangelicalism whose primary interest declares God's glory to the nations, while defending the faith, and standing in the gap for the marginalized and exploited.

I'm not completely sure that I'll succeed at an attempt to define evangelicalism, but I feel like we are at a crossroad in the United States. If the trend of the rapid decline of Christianity in America remains constant, then our faith stands in jeopardy. This is not meant to be fear-mongering. Rather, we need to wake up to the reality that "When Evangelicals sneeze, the global church catches a cold." Let's be sure that we are spreading the right virus

CHAPTER 1

WHO DEFINES EVANGELICALISM?

I remember as a child looking through a kaleidoscope. As I turned the cylinder while staring at a light, the seemingly infinite number of designs were captivating and entertaining. While evangelicalism might not be as captivating and entertaining as a kaleidoscope, it certainly seems to have an infinite number of expressions. Its mere geographical breadth and historic focus on an indigenous manifestation of Christianity helps us see how truly culturally diverse evangelicalism has become. Evangelicalism finds some form in nearly every country of the world (Cooper, 2018) as well as among the majority of the more than 10,000 distinct ethnic groups living in them.

Data Gatherer	People Groups	Unreached People Groups (UPG)	Unengaged Unreached People Groups (UUPG)
Joshua Project	16,842	6,989	
People Groups (IMB)	11,741	7,076	3,054
Finishing the Task			225

Table 1: UUPG Statistics by Organization

Historically speaking, evangelicalism can be dated to the 16th century Reformation. It has no founder *per se*, but its expression is seen in a movement of Christians with a gospel focus and passion for its proclamation. Today, evangelicals from 126 countries are loosely united in an organization known as the World Evangelical Alliance (WEA) with the following statement of faith:

> **The Holy Scriptures** *as originally given by God, divinely inspired, infallible, entirely trustworthy; and the supreme authority in all matters of faith and conduct.*

> **One God,** *eternally existent in three persons, Father, Son and Holy Spirit.*

> **Our Lord Jesus Christ,** *God manifest in the flesh, His virgin birth, His sinless human life, His divine miracles, His vicarious and atoning death, His bodily resurrection, His ascension, His mediatorial work, and his personal return in power and glory.*

> **The Salvation** *of lost and sinful man through the shed blood of the Lord Jesus Christ by faith apart from works, and regeneration by the Holy Spirit.*

> **The Holy Spirit** *by whose indwelling the believer is enabled to live a holy life, to witness and work for the Lord Jesus Christ.*

> **The Unity of the Spirit** *of all true believers, the Church, the Body of Christ.*

__The Resurrection__ of both the saved and the lost; they that are saved unto the resurrection of life, they that are lost unto the resurrection of damnation.

(Source:https://worldea.org/en/who-we-are/statement-of-faith/)

With nearly 45,000 denominations and organizations that might fit into a broad classification of what it means to be evangelical (Johnson and Zurlo, 2020), scholars struggle with defining a specific evangelical identity as we truly see a kaleidoscope of theological and ecclesiological expressions. From those in the Reformation tradition (Lutherans, Calvinists) and the Anabaptist tradition (Baptists, Mennonites) to those in the Pentecostal one (Holiness, Assembly), combined with cultural particularities of each, finding a unifying definition remains nearly an impossible task.

So, as I attempt to embark on this impossible task, let's first look at where we find evangelicals today. Then, we'll ask the question of their presence in the Bible. Finally, I'll describe the American kaleidoscope of evangelicalism.

As we continue in search of an evangelicalism, each subsequent chapter will offer some clarity and challenge some suppositions, even ponder if God might be done with the American evangelical church. Ultimately, we will return to the Bible, specifically what Jesus says should characterize a church that myopically focuses on God's mission to declare His glory to every people group on the planet. In essence, the *euangelion,* good news, stands at the very heart of anything called evangelical.

WHERE ARE EVANGELICALS?

While Christianity makes up about 1/3 of the world's population (approximately 2.4 billion people in 7,153 ethnic groups according to the Joshua Project), the Pew Research Center suggested that there were as many as 869 million people worldwide who identify with some form of evangelicalism in 2011 (Pew Research Center) while French researcher Sebastian Fath estimates the number at about 660 million in 2019 (Evangelical Focus, 2020). Reporting on Fath's research, Evangelical Focus writes,

> *Asia has the highest number of evangelical Christians: **215 million**. China (66 million), India (28), Indonesia (16), Philippines (13) and South Korea (9) are the countries with the biggest evangelical communities.*

> *Africa comes next, with **185 million** evangelicals, with Nigeria (58 million), Kenya (20), Ethiopia (18), DRC Congo (15) and South Africa (15) leading the numbers.*

> *South America has, according the estimates, **123 million** evangelicals: 47 million in Brazil, and 5 million in Argentina and 5 in Guatemala.*

> *North America has **107 million** evangelical believers: 93 in the US, 10 in Mexico and 4 in Canada.*

Europe *counts* ***23 million*** *evangelical Christians, with United Kingdom (5 million), Russia (2), Ukraine (2), Romania (2) and Germany (2) in the first positions.*

Finally, ***Oceania*** *counts* ***7 million*** *evangelicals (3 in Australia, 2 in Papua New Guinea and 1 in New Zealand).*

Fath's analysis represent an unquestionably hopeful sign for global evangelicalism. We should fully expect to see those numbers grow as the gospel continues to spread and indeed evangelical growth appears in many countries (see Table 2).

Rank	Country	Ann Gr*
1	Iran	19.6%
2	Afghanistan	16.7%
3	Gambia, The	8.9%
4	Cambodia	8.8%
5	Greenland	8.4%
6	Algeria	8.1%
7	Somalia	8.1%
8	Mongolia	7.9%
9	Kuwait	7.3%
10	Tajikistan	6.9%
11	Laos	6.8%
12	Mauritania	6.7%
13	Sao Tome & Principe	6.5%
14	Sudan	6.4%
15	Suriname	6.3%
16	Guinea-Bissau	6.2%
17	Senegal	6.1%
18	Korea, North	6.0%
19	Colombia	6.0%

20	Andorra	5.9%
21	Oman	5.9%
22	Israel	5.6%
23	San Marino	5.6%
24	Nicaragua	5.5%
25	United Arab Emirates	5.5%
26	Mozambique	5.4%
27	Nepal	5.3%
28	Equatorial Guinea	5.3%
29	Montenegro	5.2%
30	Libya	5.2%
31	Yemen	5.1%
32	Ecuador	4.9%
33	Belize	4.8%
34	Tunisia	4.7%
35	Togo	4.7%
36	Egypt	4.6%
37	Liberia	4.6%
38	Albania	4.6%
39	Luxembourg	4.6%
40	Bolivia	4.6%

Table 2: Countries where evangelicalism grows the fastest (Source: Operation World)

However, there are signs of evangelicalism's decline in other parts of the world (see Table 3). Of course, there are many factors for the decline including a decrease in birth rate in traditionally Protestant countries, an increase in immigration from the majority world where Catholicism, Islam, Hinduism, and Buddhism are predominate, as well as the global growth of what Joshua Packard called the religiously "dones" (2015).

Rank	Country	Ann Gr
1	Niue	-4.1%
2	Sweden	-0.6%
3	Georgia	-0.6%
4	Japan	-0.4%
5	Slovenia	-0.2%
6	Tokelau Islands	-0.1%
7	Falkland Islands	-0.1%
8	Finland	-0.1%
9	United Kingdom	0.0%
10	Cocos (Keeling) Islands	0.0%
11	Saint Pierre & Miquelon	0.0%
12	Palestine	0.0%
13	Denmark	0.2%
14	Swaziland	0.2%
15	Czech Republic	0.3%
16	US Virgin Islands	0.3%
17	Tonga	0.4%
18	Saint Helena	0.5%
19	Estonia	0.5%
20	New Zealand	0.5%
21	Croatia	0.5%
22	Netherlands	0.6%
23	Bermuda	0.6%
24	Guam	0.6%
25	Bulgaria	0.7%
26	Korea, South	0.7%
27	Grenada	0.7%
28	Samoa	0.7%
29	Barbados	0.8%
30	USA	0.8%
31	Canada	0.8%
32	Hungary	0.8%

33	Micronesia	0.9%
34	Germany	0.9%
35	Guyana	1.0%
36	Norway	1.0%
37	Australia	1.1%
38	Portugal	1.1%
39	Switzerland	1.2%
40	Botswana	1.2%

Table 3: Nations where evangelicalism grows the slowest or declining (Source: Operation World)

According to the US Census Bureau (2019), the current population growth rate in the United States has fallen to less than a million for the first time in 10 years. With decreasing numbers of births and increasing numbers of deaths, the population growth rate slowed to around 0.5 percent in 2019. One might be tempted to think that the 0.8 percent growth rate of evangelicalism in the United States is positive as it suggests an increase in the share of the religious economy. However, these numbers have to be kept in tension with the overall numbers of Christianity in the United States.

No doubt, the absolute numbers of evangelicals have grown in the US among certain population. For example, the growth of evangelicalism has been predominately focused in the Hispanic community. In 2014, 19 percent of Hispanics identified as evangelical whereas in 2013 only 16 percent identified as evangelicals (US Religious Landscape Survey). In 2019, *Christianity Today* reported that Latino immigrants are evangelizing the United States. In contrast, the White evangelical community, according to Robert Jones (2019), represented 21 percent of the population in 2010, whereas in 2019 that number declined to 15 percent. All this to say that it does appear evangelicalism has positive growth in certain segments of the US population while negative growth in others.

The nominal growth and decline of evangelicalism in the US and other predominately Protestant countries begs the question of whether or not this is truly evangelicalism or if it has become more of an evangelical tradition rather than an evangelical movement. Whatever it may be called, it certainly does not resemble the growth of Christianity in the early church. So, we pose the question, "were there evangelicals in the Bible?"

WERE THERE EVANGELICALS IN THE BIBLE?

The Bible might be a good place to start when attempting a definition of evangelical. After all, every Christian denomination in the world would claim that they are the correct manifestation of the church, at least as they would interpret the Bible. The problem remains, we would be hard pressed to say that there were evangelicals in the Bible, just like we would be hard pressed to say that there were Protestants, Catholics, Coptics, or Orthodox. The uniqueness and diversity of evangelicalism's contemporary expressions must beg the question of who can actually define it. That is, who has the right to put a definition on a term with so many different manifestations.

Undeniably the idea of "evangelical" originates in the Bible. Etymologically, evangelical finds its roots in the Greek word *euangelion*, simply translated good news. We will discuss this term further in chapter 5. For now, in as much as evangelicalism concerns itself with the proclamation of the good news, namely the assertion that an historically identifiable Savior came into the world (Luke 2; John 1) with a message from God (John 17:1) that He desires all people to come to the knowledge of truth (1 Tim 2:4) and be transformed from an allegiance to their own self-glorification (Rom 3:23) to an allegiance to the one true God (Acts 17:30), then we might correctly say that there were evangelicals in the Bible in spite of the apparent anachronism.

When we consider the exponential growth of the early church, we might be tempted to say that there were evangelicals in the first four centuries. After all, one would expect a religious group bearing the moniker evangelical to actually evangelize. This certainly happened prior to the politicization of Christianity in 323 AD.

The issue with suggesting there were evangelicals in the Bible lies in the fact that the context in which definitions of evangelical occur today is distinctly different from the context of the first century. First, while there were a set of Scriptures in the first century church, namely the Hebrew Scriptures, today's evangelical places a primacy on the New Testament as the expression of the new covenant revealed in Jesus Christ (Heb 8:13). The New Testament, subsequently, helps to clarify what the Christian tradition has called the Old Testament. However, the first Christians did not have the privilege of a book called the New Testament and relied upon the transmission of the teaching of the apostles; what the Apostle Paul called "traditions" (2 Thess 2:15; 1 Cor 11:2).

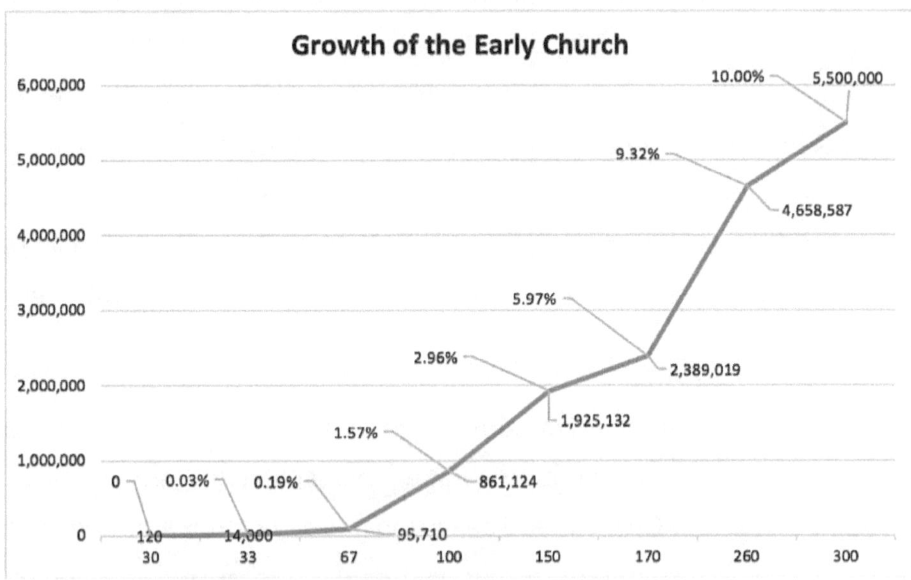

Graph 1: Growth of Early Christianity (Cooper and Till 2020)

Some evangelicals might find it difficult to appreciate that the Catholic Church finally determined the canon of the New Testament at the Council of Trent in the 16th century. This Counter Reformation to Martin Luther's (an early evangelical) Reformation sought to address his low view of several books of the New Testament (Hebrews, James, Jude, Revelation) and set the corpus of the 27 New Testament books once and for all.

No doubt, evangelicals are keen to argue that the Muratorian fragment demonstrated an early corpus of the New Testament. This 7th century Latin fragment translated from a Greek manuscript dated in the second century contains most of the New Testament books we have today. Nevertheless, the fragment aligns more closely with Luther's version of the New Testament than with our current one. Still, Athanasius of Alexandria, most famous for his defense of the nature of Christ at the first ecumenical council, composed a canon of the 27 books of the New Testament in 367 AD. Yet, his canon was not generally accepted by the universal church. All this to say that the church most definitely possessed what we call the New Testament as early as the second century, but consensus did not occur until the 16th century.

Second, the sundry expressions of church in the 21st century raises serious questions of whether or not an evangelical identity might be found in the first Christians. The various ideas of church governance (Episcopal, Presbyterian, Congregational), the form of baptism (sprinkling, immersion), and the meaning of the Lord's supper (Transubstantiation, Consubstantiation, Memorial) are all held by different Christians including some evangelicals. All support their various ecclesiological traditions from Scripture. So, is there one, unified understanding of the church? Apparently, after 21 centuries we are still unable to answer this question.

Third, there does not appear to be clear agreement for the purpose of the church. There are some evangelicals who believe that social justice sums up the purpose of the church. God is, after all, a just god who demands us "to do justice, and to love kindness, and to walk humbly with your God" (Micah 6:8). Others are just as adamant about an apologetic of the faith. Peter himself said, "always be prepared to make a defense [*apologian*] to anyone who asks you for a reason for the hope that is in you" (1 Peter 3:15). Finally, there are those who see the social justice advocates as leaning too far to a social gospel while the apologists lean too far to the modernists and point to gospel proclamation as the sole mission of the evangelical. After all, Jesus Himself commanded, "Go, make disciples of all nations" (Matt 28:18).

So, were there evangelicals in the Bible? Perhaps, but wholly unlike the kaleidoscopic evangelicalism we see today.

THE AMERICAN KALEIDOSCOPE OF EVANGELICALISM

I think the image of a kaleidoscope best describes contemporary evangelicalism. If indeed there are 45,000 evangelical denominations and organizations as suggested by the World Christian Database, then a fantastic mosaic of diversity among those who share a similar heritage exists. Yet, beyond the diversity observed in the number of denominations, a diversity in theology occurs as well. This is not the place to discuss Reformed or covenant theology, Arminian theology, dispensationalism, or Free Grace Theology. Instead, the manner in which we interpret evangelicalism remains of particular importance; what some might call a hermeneutical key for understanding evangelicalism.

Granted, one might object and say that these various theologies act as hermeneutical keys, and I'd agree. They emerge in certain contexts and cultures that influenced their particular theological positions. However, can a key be divorced from theological positions that are culturally constrained? In other words, can evangelicalism be reduced to a core, not in a reductionistic manner, but in a manner where the impact of cultural peculiarities, like nationalism, diminishes its influence on our understanding? The degree to which we are able to achieve such an evangelicalism will be measured by the degree to which we willingly hold our theologies with open hands in honest recognition that they are humanly constructed devices not divine dogma.

Allow me to illustrate this issue. The Evangelical Free Church of America's rich history in the prophetic movement of the early 1900s informed the development of an eschatological position known as premillennialism. For many years, if not decades, after the formation of the EFCA in 1950, most premillennialists were also pretribulationalists. However, the fact that there are many views of the tribulation, such specificity did not make it into the EFCA statement of faith (SOF). For an individual to be considered for ordination in the EFCA, it was enough that he held to a premillennial view of the return of Christ, among other doctrines. In 2008, discussions around changing this doctrinal position began and ultimately transformed the denomination from a staunchly premillennial position to one that recognized good evangelicals land on many sides of the eschatological debate.

Here's the issue. For more than half a century, well-qualified pastoral candidates who applied for ordination to the EFCA yet held a different view on the return of Christ were not permitted to be ordained for gospel ministry as they were considered in doctrinal error. Now, however, with the change of the SOF, they would no longer be considered in doctrinal error. Yet, who decides this? Did God decide in 1950 that those who did not agree with the SOF were in doctrinal error and now He changed His mind to allow those who were once in error to be ordained? You see how ridiculous some theological arguments can get and why such theological points must be held loosely.

Near the end of his life in the middle of the fifth century, Augustine of Hippo began to write a commentary on the book of Genesis. He never completed it, but what he realized as he worked on it should inform our judgment of those who do not agree with us on points of theology. He writes,

In matters that are obscure and far beyond our vision, even in such as we may find treated in Holy Scripture, different interpretations are sometimes possible without prejudice to the faith we have received. In such a case, we should not rush in headlong and so firmly take our stand on one side that, if further progress in search of truth justly undermines this position, we too fall with it. (The Literal Meaning of Genesis 1.18)

Early in his career, Augustine would have hardly written such lines as he held strongly to his theological positions. Perhaps as he matured as a theologian and apologist for the faith he realized that all of our theological opinions are ill-fated human attempts to explain the un-explainable. Nevertheless, in the 21st century we find ourselves in this evangelical kaleidoscope. As it keeps turning, new views will emerge and draw their clear lines of distinction from other evangelicals.

As I have been wrestling with this kaleidoscope idea, it seems to me that there are a number of cultural factors that have contributed to forming an evangelical identity or perhaps multiple evangelical identities in the United States. These factors often compete with one another and are not necessarily bound by ecclesiastical limits or doc-trinal statements. At times, they are united by political affiliations and take on more of a philosophical, even ideological bent to their identity. Let me briefly unpack at least four of those by first setting the limits of the ideologies and then working toward the middle.

On one side of the limit, modern-day evangelicalism draws its roots from the fundamentalist movement at the turn of the 20th century. Growing out of a deepening conviction that science and intellectualism threatened Christianity, fundamentalists drew lines in the sand in regards to what were believed to be fundamentals of the faith. The so-called fundamentalist-modernist debate focused on the preservation of core doctrines of creation, Scripture, and the work of Jesus Christ (His historicity, death, resurrection, and atoning work of salvation). As the debate heightened, fundamentalists were per-ceived to be anti-intellectual as they ignored scientific enquiry and current scientific advancement while holding tightly to a literal inter-pretation of the Bible.

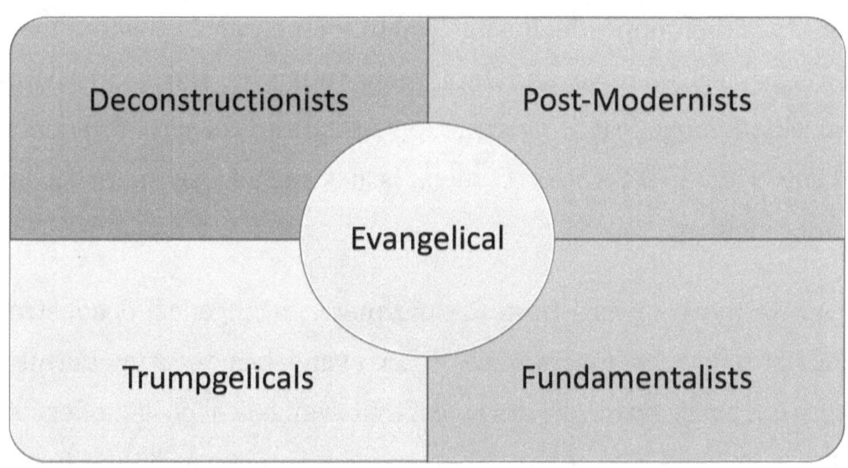

Diagram 1: The kaleidoscope of evangelicalism

On the other side of the limit, evangelical deconstructionists find their roots in what has been mistakenly called post-modernism. Grounded in the Enlightenment idea of human autonomy, evangelical deconstructionists view a Christianity laden with misinterpretation and misrepresentation. To them, the current Christian expression emerges out of a misogynistic, patriarchal heritage to control what people believed. Some doctrines, particularly those surrounding humanity and Scripture, are archaic leftovers of a hegemonic Christianity and are open for re-interpretation. What that re-interpretation means, is largely left to the interpreter. Evangelical deconstructionists tend to lean toward a form of liberation theology as well as to feminism.

Politically speaking, the perimeter of evangelicalism stands acutely divided. In fact, as fundamentalists and deconstructionists look at each other, they are more likely to not see anything evangelical in the identity of their opposite. Evangelical fundamentalists position themselves as conservative and find their values in the 1980s Moral Majority. Evangelical deconstructionism falls to the left of the political spectrum as it focuses on social issues such as gay marriage and gender identity.

As we move inward from the perimeter, evangelical deconstructionism might be moderated by an evangelical post-modernism. There is a place, however, to suggest that evangelical post-modernism actually appears well before deconstructionism just as it does in both architecture and art. An evangelical post-modernism, which we will discuss further in chapter 10, focuses on recovering the historical understanding of Christianity as articulated in the Apostolic and Church Fathers of the first six centuries.

Finally, as we move inward from evangelical fundamentalism we come to the subject of the next chapter. The neologism "Trumpgelical" distinctly expresses a form of fundamentalism with obvious nationalistic tendencies. Trumpgelicals are given a dedicated treatment largely due to their voice in the current US religious climate. Of the four ideologies I've briefly described, Trumpgelicals have garnered the most attention in the media and popular culture as their prominent spokespeople have vast resources and networks around the country. Ostensibly, over the past four years, they have also caused the most confusion around the identity of evangelicals who have been touted as the largest voting block in America.

In contrast, few evangelicals will have heard of many Democratic efforts to identify as evangelical, although those attempts have been made in what I called evangelical deconstructionism. Progressive evangelicals, like those represented by Vote Common Good espouse a platform to prevent the re-election of Trump. While not necessarily aligned with any political party or evangelical deconstructionism, they claim to be:

Inspiring, energizing, and mobilizing people of faith to make the common good their voting criteria and to pursue faith, hope, & love for a change on election day 2020 and prevent the re-election of Donald Trump. (http://votecommongood.com)

In the middle but not uninfluenced by the other ideologies, is where, I believe, we will find a contemporary definition of evangelicalism. To that end we head in the next eleven chapters. First, let's try to understand this neologism: Trumpgelical.

***

These are confusing times. The conflation of religion and politics is seen all across the evangelical spectrum. For example, in an attempt to explain the balance between nationalism and Christianity, John Piper stated,

The reason I think it's good to have special affections for these particular attachments [countries, states, cities] is that the Bible seems to point in that direction in several ways. For example,

Paul says in Galatians 6:10, "As we have opportunity, let us do good to everyone, and especially to those who are of the household of faith." So, it's as though there is this specialness about those who are close to you and like you. There is a kind of affection for them that's different. (2020)

This type of patriotic hermeneutic betrays a tendency to interpret Scripture through the lens of a nationalistic identity resulting in a belief that the Christian can share two identities. Granted, Piper, who did not support Clinton or Trump in the 2016 election, continues and clarifies that the affection one has for their country or culture should not outweigh one's affection for Christ. Nevertheless, the actions of many American evangelicals demonstrate a fogginess to their identity. They reveal the innate ability for the human mind to hold two opposite convictions in tension. So, for instance, an American evangelical might be able to support the deportation of illegal aliens in the name of American economic and security interests while holding the conviction of welcoming the stranger among them (Deut 10:19).

I believe we are at a crucial moment in the history of American evangelicalism. The lines of differences are becoming increasingly distinct just as the lines delineating the various shapes and sizes of the images in a kaleidoscope. It remains incumbent on those of us who are looking through the kaleidoscope – students of culture and Christianity – to assess what we see and attempt to move us forward to a place where we can all say, "this is us" without the confusion and conflation of identities. I hope this current attempt will help us on the journey.

CHAPTER 2

TRUMPGELICALISM: A FOUR-YEAR VIRUS

For years, I researched what are known in the academic world as New Religious Movements (NRMs); religions like Mormons, Jehovah's Witnesses, Wicca, and Druidry. To many evangelicals and others, NRMs are pejoratively known as cults, those so-called deviant religious expressions that stray from the majority religion of a country. While the study of NRMs has largely focused on the Western world and the various new spiritualities that have emerged mostly out of Christianity, there is also a place for their study in other parts of the globe where there are deviant expressions of Islam, Hinduism, and Buddhism.

One area of growing interest in the study of religious expressions is the coalescing of faith and politics. Obviously not unique as religion has played an important role in politics since ancient times, even among God's chosen people. One might recall Israel's desire to be like other nations and have a political leader, "Now appoint for us a king to judge us like all the nations" (1 Samuel 8:5). At times, religion has been used as a scapegoat for the justification of a particular political expression. The Marxist adage, while it might be true, "religion is the opium of the masses," was used to suppress faith expressions. No doubt, religion takes on a whole new identity when combined with politics and gives political leaders legitimacy to enact typically nationalistic agendas. This was certainly the case in the first century AD as the Roman Empire hailed Caesar as a god and the Jews expected his overthrow under the leadership of a political messiah.

This phenomenon of conflating faith and politics occurs in our day as well where political leaders use religion to direct their policies for nationalistic purposes. For example, in India, Prime Minister Narendra Modi uses Hindu nationalism to legitimize his immigration policy. In so doing, he successfully suppresses other faith expressions (namely Islam and Christianity). Similarly, Russia's president Vladimir Putin aligns himself with the Russian Orthodox Church in order to garner support as a patriotic leader who has now been in office longer than Joseph Stalin.

In the United States, we see something comparable in the emergence of a New American Religion where faith and politics conflate. Perhaps, one might argue, this conflation encompasses the tradition of an older American religion that began with the Rev. Jerry Falwell's Moral Majority in the 1970s and flourished during the presidency of Ronald Reagan. However, this new expression and its primary leader appear to have much more in common with NRMs. For the sake of clarity, I call this New American Religion "Trumpgelicalism." I do not mean this as derogatory, but as a distinction from a historical under-standing of evangelicalism.

In 1989, David Bebbington summarized an historical understanding of evangelicalism in his quadrilateral, qualities that characterized evangelicalism in Great Britain and perhaps in the United States as well: Biblicism, Crucicentrism, Conversionism, and Activism (Bebbington, 1989). In 1995, Alister McGrath outlined this historic evangelical faith with the six following markers that we will discuss later in chapter 8:

1. The supreme authority of Scripture as a source of knowledge of God and a guide to Christian living.
2. The majesty of Jesus Christ, both as incarnate God and Lord, and as the Savior of sinful humanity.
3. The lordship of the Holy Spirit.
4. The need for personal conversion.
5. The priority of evangelism for both individual Christians and the church as a whole.
6. The importance of the Christian community for spiritual nourishment, fellowship and growth. (McGrath, 1995: 55-56)

Before we get to an historical understanding of evangelicalism, we'll turn our attention to a New American Religion.

DEFINING TRUMPGELICALISM

Trumpgelicalism might be described as a body of adherents to the political and social policies of the 45th President of the United States, Donald J. Trump. Such policies take on a distinctly religious flavor as they are mixed with certain values of evangelicalism as expressed originally by the Moral Majority. Those adherents to Trumpgelicalism are commonly politically and socially conservative. They champion the sanctity of human life, but only in regards to the rights of the unborn as they tend to support capital punishment, homicide in the case of protecting personal property, terrorist assassinations, and war in just causes. They are pro-guns and support the right to bear weapons in public. Trumpgelicals are mostly White and hold to a Judeo-Christian ethic that is often conflated with the US Constitution and Declaration of Independence. They are deeply nationalistic which influences their views on immigration and the right to citizenship of illegal immigrants as well as national border security. They are also strongly pro-Israel which conforms to a form of eschatological dispensationalism.

Trumpgelicals rally around their collective animosity for former presidents, especially democratic ones, but not exclusively. They tolerate the immorality of the current president – grabbing the genitals of women, relationships with prostitutes and a human trafficker, use of vulgar language, cyber bullying, narcissistic pursuit of personal interests, and racial epitaphs – and excuse it as the acts of a sinful person, which of course we all are. After all, many claim that the conservative social and political policies protecting Christianity from the ostensibly liberalization of an America socialism merits turning the other cheek to clearly unbiblical actions more aligned with debauchery and licentiousness.

Not surprisingly, due to Trump's actions, fewer than half of Americans believe he is Christian (Fahmy, 2020). In spite of that, Matthew Teague, a *Guardian* reporter, noted the perspective of one Trumpgelical, "[Southern Baptist Pastor Robert] Jeffress sees no conflict between Trump's behavior and the Bible he held up on Monday evening [at St. John's Episcopal Church near the Whitehouse]. 'You mean, does he pretend to be perfectly pious?' he said. 'No'" (Teague, 2020).

	Clinton (%)	Trump (%)
Protestant/other Christian	39	58
Catholic	45	52
White Catholic	37	60
Hispanic Catholic	67	26
Jewish	71	24
Other faiths	62	29
Religiously unaffiliated	68	26
White, born-again/evangelical	16	81
Mormon	25	61

Table 4: Presidential vote by religious affiliation and race (Pew Research 2016)

Trumpgelicals include well-known evangelicals such as the aforementioned Robert Jeffress, as well as Jerry Falwell, Jr., James

Dobson, Franklin Graham, Eric Metaxas, Paula White (who is credited with leading Trump to Christ), and others (see table 5). However, they are not exclusively White evangelicals. In 2016, White Catholics overwhelmingly supported the Trump presidency over Hillary Clinton's bid by 60 to 37 percent.

Now, let me be clear. Not everyone who supports Trump are Trumpgelicals. Some who voted for Trump in the 2016 general election argued that he was the lesser of two evils, an idea that seems to motivate the voting habits of many since the Clinton presidency. Consider, for example, Wayne Grudem's (2016) ardent defense for voting Trump. The article, "Why Voting for Donald Trump is a Morally Good Choice," concludes with his reasoned argument, "The most likely result of voting for Trump is that he will govern the way he promises to do, bringing much good to the nation." However, one would hardly conclude that Grudem is a Trumpgelical, at least I assume he is not.

TRUMPGELICALISM'S SIMILARITIES WITH NRMS

Trumpgelicals are a distinct group of people who believe that America is a Christian country and see their duty to the country in passing legislation addressing their moral views presumably aligned with their interpretation of the Bible. In this sense, while not necessarily as deviant from the historic Christian faith like Mormonism or Jehovah's Witnesses, there is little doubt that Trumpgelicalism shares many features with new religious movements (NRMs). In 1993, James Beckford enumerated the features common to NRMs that continue to hold true today:

- Many NRMs have singular ideologies which draw upon exotic or unusual values and assumptions.
- The "enrollment economies" of most NRMs are based on the recruitment of young, well educated, productive, healthy, middle-class adults.
- There is a tendency for NRMs to aspire to total control over their participants' lives.
- NRMs are "greedy institutions" which experience a high rate of turnover in members and a strong sense of opposition from some apostates.
- There is intense organized opposition to controversial NRMs.
- The founder-leaders of NRMs tend to enjoy a high profile and autocratic powers.
- A few NRMs have generated massive wealth.
- The number of people directly affected by NRMs is very small. The cultural influence of the movements has also been slight. But their profile in the mass media is disproportionately alarmist and demonic. (Beckford, 1993)

How do Trumpgelicals compare to NRMs? First, ideologically speaking, the president's political platform directly appeals to his followers. With crowds chanting such "singular ideologies" as "build that wall" and "lock her up," as well as his pro-life, pro-conservative justices, and pro-Christian platforms, Trump strategically laid out his "values and assumptions" knowing full well that he would gain support among politically conservative White evangelicals, one of the largest voting blocks in America. These Trumpgelicals believe Christianity is attacked by the political left, immigrants, and Hillary Clinton, and feel as if their American dream is threatened.

Second, even though the news media and Democratic pundits claim that Trump supporters are not "young, well-educated, productive, healthy, middle-class adults," the fact remains, many are. As Angela Denker (2020) noted, "Although Trump's crowds are often depicted by mainstream media as undereducated, rural, blue-collar, rough-around-the-edges type folks, [23 year-old Dominic] Cassella says Thomas More [College of Liberal Arts] students, with their polished exterior and traditional commitment to intellectualism, fit right in." Indeed, many of Trump's evangelical supporters are very well educated. For example, Eric Metaxas graduated from Yale University, Robert Jeffress graduated from Baylor University and holds a Doctor of Ministry from Southwestern Baptist Theological Seminary, and James Dobson earned a Doctor of Philosophy from the University of Southern California.

Third, Trump's demands for loyalty – the idea of total control – will certainly be a marker of his presidency (Kruse, 2018). This demand for loyalty became infamous in his relationship with former FBI director James Comey. His control manifests in a sort of a quid pro quo; that is, he will do something for you – hold the Bible on the steps of St. John's Episcopal Church, for example – and you will do something for him – namely, vote him into a second term. As Teague (2020) noted, "The Horbowys had gathered in Tallahassee, Florida, to watch live as Trump walked from the White House to St John's. 'My mother just shouted out, "God give him strength! He's doing a Jericho walk!"'' A "Jericho walk" alludes to the biblical reference when Israel circumnavigated the city of Jericho, eventually blew their trumpets, and the walls fell down (Joshua 6:1-27).

	2017 (%)	2019 (%)
Protestant	52	50
White mainline Protestant	49	48
White, born-again/evangelical	78	69
Catholic	36	36
White Catholic	52	44
Non-white Catholic	13	26
Other faiths	62	29
Religiously unaffiliated	24	20

Table 5: White evangelical Protestants consistently give President Trump high marks (Pew Research Center 2019)

Fourth, leaders of new religions tend to be polarizing figures, something endemic to the Trump presidency. At the same time, as we get deeper into the 2020 election cycle, we are beginning to see a "high-rate of turnover" among Trump supporters. As of June 2020, the president is experiencing an unprecedented disapproval rating (58-60 percent) as well as disapproval over his handling of current societal challenges. In regards to his handling of COVID-19, 58 percent disapprove, and of his handling of racial stresses, 63 percent believe Trump made tensions worse. As a result, evangelical support has begun to wane as has his support from other religious groups. However, true Trumpgelicals are comparable to wine tasters who are myopically loyal due to their financial investment in a bottle of vintage wine indifferent to the taste. Trumpgelicals tend to be biased due to the political and emotional investment to their ideology. We'll discuss the comparison between wine tasters and political pundits in chapter 4.

	March (%)	April (%)	May (%)
White mainline Protestant	62	44	51
White, born-again/evangeli-cal	77	66	62
Non-white Protestant	40	36	40
White Catholic	60	48	37
Religiously un-affiliated	36	37	34

Table 6: Trump's favorability among religious groups (PRRI, 2020)

Fifth, the intense organized opposition to Trump appears in the news every day. Not only is this opposition against the president, but evangelicals have also seen a significant decline in numbers due in some measure to their support for Trump. In the 1960s to 1980s, evangelicalism enjoyed a growing popularity in the United States owed largely to Billy Graham. However, Robert Jones (2019) notes that White evangelical Protestants have shrunk from 21 percent of the US population in 2010 to 15 percent in 2019. Even though Trumpgelicals represent fewer than 15 percent of the adult population, their notoriety in the media is disproportionally exaggerated as Beckford observed in other NRMs.

Sixth, as a New American Religion, Trumpgelicalism is more of a movement of various evangelicals rather than an organization of adherents like we observed in the 1970s and 80s with the Moral Majority. As such, we find it difficult to calculate the financial impact of Trumpgelicalism. Yet, clearly Trumpgelical surrogates account for a significant share of personal wealth in the United States.

Trumpgelical	Estimated Net Worth (USD)
Robert Jeffress	$17 million
Paula White	$6 million
Franklin Graham	$12 million
Jerry Falwell, Jr.	$10 million

Table 7: Estimated Net Worth of Selected Trumpgelicals (Source: The Wealth Record)

Such similarities between Trumpgelicals and new religious movements demand an evangelicalism distinct, even distant, from this politically and socially charged New American Religion. That is the purpose of this book. As we continue through what might be described as the most interesting period of human history, certainly the most challenging in our lifetimes, we recognize an imperative to rediscover and restore evangelical identity. Perhaps we might call this a counter-intuitive reformation of contemporary evangelicalism, a potential cure for a plague infecting the American church.

***

It seems obvious that the salient feature of Trumpgelicalism is its conflation of conservative Republican politics with Christianity. This conflation continues to perpetuate the myth of America as a Christian nation. Certainly, the United States was founded with Judeo-Christian values as a place where people had freedom to express their religious beliefs. No argument there. However, the idea of a Christian nation stands antithetical to the biblical understanding of the kingdom of God. Equally, such a political theology would not have been expressed by the founding fathers of the United States. In fact, Article 11 of the Treaty of Tripoli, which was ratified by the United States Senate on June 7, 1797 and signed by President John Adams, clearly declared the following:

As the Government of the United States of America is not, in any sense, founded on the Christian religion; as it has in itself no character of enmity against the laws, religion, or tranquility, of Mussulmen [Muslims]; and as the said States never entered into any war or act of hostility against any Mahometan [Islamic] nation, it is declared by the parties that no pretext arising from religious opinions shall ever produce an interruption of the harmony existing between the two countries.

Instead of conflating faith and politics, Trumpgelicals might consider the early church. Those faithful disciples had no intention of becoming a nation, and Jesus, including His apostles, had no political ambitions. They were a community with a singular focus: declaring the glory of God to all people equally and without discrimination. So, in the next chapter, we'll examine the apolitical nature of Jesus. Perhaps this is the starting point to an evangelical identity in the context of this New American Religion, racial tensions, and a global pandemic.

President Trump's Evangelical Advisory Board	
Gary Bauer	President, American Values; former president of Family Research Council; former chief domestic policy adviser in the Reagan administration
Mark Burns	Co-founder and CEO of The NOW Television Network in Easley, S.C.; spoke at the 2016 Republican National Convention
Tim Clinton	President, American Association of Christian Counselors
James Dobson	Author, psychologist and host, "Family Talk"
Jordan Easley	Pastor of Englewood Baptist Church in Jackson, Tenn.; chairs Southern Baptists' Young Leaders Advisory Council
Jerry Falwell Jr.	President, Liberty University in Lynchburg, Va.
Ronnie Floyd	Author and senior pastor, Cross Church in northwest Arkansas; former Southern Baptist Convention president
Jack Graham	Author and pastor of Prestonwood Baptist Church in Plano, Texas; former Southern Baptist Convention president
Rodney Howard-Browne	Co-founder of The River at Tampa Bay Church and Revival Ministries International in Florida
Harry Jackson	Senior pastor, Hope Christian Church in Beltsville, Md.; co-founder of The Reconciled Church: Healing the Racial Divide

Robert Jeffress	Senior pastor, First Baptist Church of Dallas; hosted Fourth of July event at Kennedy Center featuring Trump as a speaker
Richard Land	President, Southern Evangelical Seminary in Matthews, N.C.; former president, Southern Baptist Convention Ethics and Religious Liberty Commission
Greg Laurie	Author and senior pastor of Harvest Christian Fellowship in Riverside, Calif.
Eric Metaxas	Author and host, "The Eric Metaxas Show"; speaker, 2012 National Prayer Breakfast
Johnnie Moore	Author, religious freedom advocate and public relations executive; serves as unofficial spokesman for group of evangelicals advising Trump administration
Frank Page	President and CEO, Southern Baptist Convention Executive Committee; former Southern Baptist Convention president; former member of President Obama's Advisory Council on Faith-based and Neighborhood Partnerships
Tony Perkins	President, Family Research Council
Ralph Reed	Founder, Faith and Freedom Coalition; former executive director, Christian Coalition
Tony Suarez	Executive vice president, National Hispanic Christian Leadership Conference
Paula White	Senior pastor, New Destiny Christian Center in Apopka, Fla.; first clergywoman to give an invocation at an inauguration

Table 8: President Trump's Evangelical Advisory Board (Source: National Catholic Reporter)

CHAPTER 3

THE POLITICS OF JESUS: A MITIGATION STRATEGY FOR EVANGELICAL DEMOCRATS AND REPUBLICANS

An aphorism attributed to the first century BC Roman orator, Marcus Cicero, goes like this, "Not to know what has been transacted in former times is to be always a child. If no use is made of the labors of past ages, the world must remain always in the infancy of knowledge." During his time, the political infighting of the Roman senate reminds us that what we see in the three branches of the US government ought not be a surprise. Even the vitriolic reaction of evangelical brothers and sisters to Mark Galli's (2019) stinging call for Trump's impeachment in a *Christianity Today* editorial should not be surprising (more about that in the next chapter). In fact, for the New Testament student, it might remind us of the politics in 1st century BC – 1st century AD Israel when Rome controlled the Judean countryside.

While it might be interesting to rehearse the entire political history of Israel prior to the construction of the second temple, what stands of particular interest is the arrival of Jesus Christ among a politically divided nation. By the time of His incarnation, the political tension in Israel felt particularly perilous. On the one side were the Herodians, a group of Jews who were theologically aligned with the Pharisees, but had more in common with the political views of the Hellenized Sadducees. On the other side, the Zealots, full of religious fervor, were a grassroots Jewish group that plotted the overthrow of the Roman government. Ultimately, neither side liked Jesus very much.

The Herodians believed that the government provided more assurance for the protection of life and property so they gladly welcomed and supported the reign of Herod the Great, who Caesar declared "King of the Jews." Herod the Great found favor among the Jews in the restoration of the temple in the second decade of the first century BC. Feeling threatened at the announcement of a new king of the Jews, he also murdered the male children of Bethlehem (Matt 2:16-18), with no apparent recourse from the Jewish citizens of the city. Herod's intentions and actions compelled the Holy Family to take refuge in Egypt until his death in 4 BC.

His successor, Herod Antipas the Tetrarch, continued to find favor among the Jews. Eventually, due to being confronted for his immoral behavior, he beheaded John the Baptist at the request of his step-daughter (Luke 9:7-9). John the Baptist, the forerunner to Christ, called people to repentance, indifferent of their political leanings, as the kingdom of God was at hand (Mark 1:15). Meanwhile, the politically entrenched Herodians joined the Pharisees in plotting to destroy Jesus after being alarmed by His powers of healing (Mark 3:6), perhaps even thinking His power was demonic (Mark 3:22). Additionally, they attempted to trick Him into taking a public stand on tax issues hoping to discredit Him as a Jewish partisan (Mark 12:17).

Possibly the religious fanatics of the day, the Zealots vehemently opposed Roman rule. Later, they would be the leaders during the Jewish Wars that resulted in the destruction of the second temple in 70 AD. Even a few of Jesus's followers – Simon the Zealot for example – were caught up in this movement. If social media would have existed, they would have certainly been known as #jewishlivesmatter. No doubt others of His disciples had similar political leanings, particularly Peter who prepared himself to die by the sword in defense of his beliefs (John 18:10) only to be humiliated when he denied the vary one he sought to defend (Matt 24:35-36).

Both the Herodians and the Zealots were Bible believing Jews and patriotic nationalists. Yet, they expressed their views in politically different ways. Both hoped for a Jewish messiah who would re-establish the glory of Israel as a political leader. While their approaches differed, neither group foresaw the incarnation of God Himself who is the Savior, not only of the Jews, but of the world (John 3:16). Jesus stepped into this politically divided Israel that appears not all that dissimilar from the United States today, perhaps not even dissimilar from the rest of the world as patriotic nationalist movements rise across the globe.

Jesus's remarkable impact on the Apostle Peter cannot be mistaken. Peter, writing from a place of a changed person, later describes Jesus's attitude toward the political and religious leaders of His day, "When he was reviled, he did not revile in return; when he suffered, he did not threaten, but continued entrusting Himself to Him who judges justly" (1 Peter 2:23). Jesus certainly challenged the system; however, He always pointed His followers to the fulfillment of God's will. It was, after all, His purpose (John 5:30; Matt 7:21). His challenge to the systemic issues came without any political affiliation – He was not a Herodian or a Zealot. Yet, it also came with an unwavering commitment to glorify His Father (John 17:1-5).

Is there a lesson we might learn from history so we do not remain a child, as Cicero insinuated, in our 21st century politically divided nation? Again, Peter reminds us,

Be subject for the Lord's sake to every human institution, whether it be to the emperor as supreme, or to governors as sent by him to punish those who do evil and to praise those who do good. For this is the will of God, that by doing good you should put to silence the ignorance of foolish people. Live as people who are free, not using your freedom as a cover-up for evil, but living as servants of God. Honor everyone. Love the brotherhood. Fear God. Honor the emperor. (1 Peter 2:13-17)

In the context of first century Christianity, Peter is not advocating a politicizing of Christ's followers or a weaponizing of Scripture to prove a point. He is not anticipating a two-party system of Republicans and Democrats. Instead, he calls us who are Christ-followers to the gentle and respectful proclamation of the good news delivered for all people (1 Peter 3:15-17). Perhaps this is too simple or naïve for our sophisticated society. After all, we are certainly more civil than the Herodians and Zealots of Jesus's day; our two-party system far superior. But how certain are we?

A MITIGATION LESSON FOR DEMOCRATS AND REPUBLICANS

In the early fifth century, the North African theologian, Augustine, understood the New Testament to teach that sometimes violent coercion of heretics and unbelievers was acceptable to ensure a Christian nation. To justify such actions toward the so-called heretical Donatists, he wrote, "You also read how he who was at first Saul, and afterwards Paul, was compelled, by the great violence with which Christ coerced him, to know and to embrace the truth" (Letter XCIII 2.5). While there is much to appreciate from this Berber theologian, acts of coercion and violence have been justified by different groups based on their understanding of "right" since the beginning of a nationalistic form of Christianity in the early 300s.

Jesus knew this all too well even in His day. Whether it was from Jewish religious leadership or Roman political leaders, acts of violence were most certainly a part of first century Palestine. He challenged such systems and His challenge caused division, but not division as we are currently witnessing in our society, particularly among evangelicals in the 21st century. The division He caused included:

- His identification as God in opposition to both Jewish and Gentile views of deities (John 10:30).
- His commitment to peace, but peace that comes through uniting with Him and not religious or political authorities (John 14:27).
- His challenge to His disciples to not lord authority over others like the Gentile leaders (Matt 20:25-26).
- And His call to stand up for justice, defend the faith, and proclaim the good news as core motivations of the church (Rev 2:1-7).

Jesus provided a new way to think about the world in which we live, a new group identity, if you will. Such an identity unites all believers indiscriminately. There is no prejudice in the body of Christ. This group identity is united in purpose, which Jesus Himself modeled for us: the glorification of God through the defense of the faith, care for the marginalized, and proclamation of the *euangelion* (i.e. good news). Perhaps Paul captures the idea of group identity best in Ephesians 2,

For he himself [Jesus] is our peace, who has made us both one [Jews and Gentiles] and has broken down in his flesh the dividing wall of hostility by abolishing the law of commandments expressed in ordinances, that he might create in himself one new [humanity] in place of the two, so making peace, and might reconcile us both to God in one body through the cross, thereby killing the hostility. And he came and preached peace to you who were far off and peace to those who were near. For through him we both have access in one Spirit to the Father. So then you are no longer strangers and aliens, but you are fellow citizens with the saints and members of the household of God. (Eph 2:14–19)

Admittedly, group identity is tremendously complicated in ethnically diverse contexts. Biologically speaking, we are one race. The nominal genetic difference between ethnicities leads us to a correct assessment that we are the human race. However, there is a different issue at play. It seems to me that what we are presently experiencing in American society is a sociological phenomenon rather than a biological one. That being said, we can legitimately talk about race – White, Brown, Black – as a social construct especially in areas where the clear ethnic lines are quite blurred like in the United States. For example, my "people" are ethnically Scottish, but I would never call myself a Scottish-American. Instead, I refer to myself as a White or Caucasian (race) American rather than as ethnically Scottish.

Simply summarized, we – White, Black, and Brown evangelicals whether Democrat or Republican – are not acting as if we are image bearers of God with a shared group identity as members of that one household Paul describes. What is more, we are certainly not doing the works for which we are created (Eph 2:10). So, one might say that societal tensions (race, politics, religion) are a symptom of a deeper problem. For the Christian, it bears the mark of the human desire to steal glory from God, a problem dating back to the Garden of Eden.

It seems to me that a principal question is how to address the human penchant to glorify itself? In other words, how do we navigate the selfish motives of a group – whether racial, ethnic, political, or religious – to work towards the group's own predisposition to better itself, even if at the expense of different groups? In addition, how does *our* group guard itself from that very same predisposition? Ultimately, how do we come to a place where, in spite of differences in race and politics, we all identify primarily with the group Jesus Himself created, the place of our true citizenship as a member of God's household?

The first steps to a common group identity have to include: 1) being present so we begin to understand other groups, 2) entering dialogue so we can clarify what we understand about each other, and 3) understanding how we arrived in our present situation. A long history of racial/ethnic as well as political tensions exists in our country and bear an incredible influence, not only on our groups, but also on the events we see today. If we cannot first be present, dialogue, and understand history we will be doomed to repeat it. This requires courageous leadership from all of us and to this subject we turn in the next chapter.

JESUS'S FAVORITE POLITICAL PARTY

Admittedly, there are those who see Jesus as very political. After all, did He not talk about a "political system" called the kingdom of God not being of this world (John 18:36)? A place where He would be King of kings (Rev 19:16)? What is more, does not entering this kingdom require a remarkable level of loyalty? We must: 1) do away with body parts that make us sin (Mark 9:47); 2) give up all our wealth (Mark 10:23); 3) be absolutely committed (Luke 9:62); 4) not worry about our future (Luke 12:31); and much more. Entering the kingdom of God represents no easy task. It demands our undivided attention because it was not Abraham Lincoln nor Ronald Reagan who said, "Every kingdom divided against itself is laid waste, and no city or house divided against itself will stand" (Matt 12:25). It was Jesus.

Yet, it is unhelpful to think of the kingdom of God in terms of humanly constructed political systems. God's kingdom does not constitute a government even though many are tempted to call it a theocracy. A theocracy, just as a democracy, demonstrates a human attempt to design a system of governance. A theocracy's difference with a democracy is that a theocracy rules by divine right. This system of governance places the power of divine judgment in the hands of a select individual or group of divine representatives; something that we see in Iran, for example. In spite of the fact that the apostles will sit on thrones to judge the tribes of Israel (Luke 22:28-30), we find no theocratic system of government indicated in Scripture.

Jesus and the early disciples were not concerned about the politic of the day, that is governmental, educational, economical, or social systems. They did not devise a political theology. Their concern landed squarely on the people caught up in those often unjust systems. To suggest they were concerned about the systems, or a political theology, makes the mission about changing the system when Jesus' mission remained about God's glory manifested in the worship of more and more people. When people are transformed then systems naturally transform. So, I hold that Jesus stood apolitical in this regard. Not dispassionate about people's situations especially where injustice ruled. Rather, He wholly focused on His Father's glory. This embodies the foundation for a Christian movement and our group's (i.e. evangelical) identity.

***

Democrats and Republicans must be careful on two fronts. First, they must regard "the other" in kindness and generosity. Both sides are not completely wrong nor are they completely right. Neither side exists solely on "truth." Second, Democrats and Republicans alike must be careful of the manner in which they apply Scripture to their political ideologies. For example, there is no space in evangelicalism for Franklin Graham and Eric Metaxas to demonize evangelical brothers and sisters for not supporting their political views (Wehner, 2019; Metaxas, 2019). Just because someone disagrees with your politics does not give you or me the right to declare they are under demonic influence. Yes, they might be correct to assert the presence of a spiritual battle, but our battle is not against flesh and blood (Eph 6:12), and the battle is always focused on the extension of God's rule not the rule of Democrats and Republicans.

Whether on the left or right of the political spectrum, any form of politicization of faith can, and has, easily turned to a weaponizing of words that inflame and divide the people of God. That does not typify the way of Jesus. Just as Jesus did not identify as a Zealot or Herodian, neither does He identify as a Democrat or Republican. Instead, as Paul reminds us, Jesus shows favor to each, "be to one another kind, compassionate, gracious to each other just as God in Christ showed graciousness to you" (Eph 4:32, my translation). We must endeavor to be like our King aligned with the group He created.

Tertullian (b. 160), writing in the late second century, articulates an early view of the Christian's relationship to the state. He clearly saw little value. In fact, he understood that such a wedding of Christianity and government was idolatrous:

There can be no compatibility between the divine and the human sacrament (military oath), the standard of Christ and the standard of the devil, the camp of light and the camp of darkness. One soul cannot serve two masters-God and Caesar. Moses, to be sure, carried a rod; Aaron wore a military belt, and John (the Baptist) is girt with leather (i.e., like a soldier); and, if you really want to play around with the subject, Joshua the son of Nun led an army and the people waged war. But how will a Christian man go to war? Indeed, how will he serve even in peacetime without a sword which the Lord has taken away? For even if soldiers came to John and received advice on how to act, and even if a centurion became a believer, the Lord, in subsequently disarming Peter, disarmed every soldier. No uniform is lawful among us if it is designated for an unlawful action. (Treatise on Idolatry 19)

Tertullian provides us something to consider as a mitigation strategy for evangelical Democrats and Republicans; even for the human race.

CHAPTER 4

LEADERSHIP, WINE TASTING AND MORE MITIGATION

When I was in my second year at Texas A&M University, our architectural design class took on a project to work with a local vineyard on a design for a new facility outside of College Station. As we began the design process, we had the vintner make a presentation on the science of winemaking. We learned about proper cultivation of grapes, whether white or red, and the timing for the harvest. He taught us about the process of crushing and pressing the grapes, then filtering the juice into proper oak casks for red or stainless-steel tanks for white. Back in the day, we were all of drinking age and you just knew that an entire class was looking forward to impressing others with their new found understanding of oenology.

More than anything the vintner taught, I was most struck by wine tasting and the fanfare that accompanied the corking of a vintage wine. From the silver-plated wine tasting cup, or tastevin, to the aroma and swirling technique, the process represents a ritual that can be quite multifarious as the taster judges the appearance, sensation in the mouth, and aftertaste. I do not think anyone in the lecture hall was prepared, however, for the vintner to admit that, more often than not, a vintage wine tasted vinegary due to bacteria coming in contact with the air and creating acetic acid. With a smirk on his face and a slight whisper, the vintner secretly confessed that no one would ever admit to the bad taste of a wine after spending as much as $2,000 for a bottle.

Doesn't that ring true of us in a politically charged society? Think about it. When our social media lights up over sundry antics in Washington D.C. and evangelicals begin to fight against evangelicals, aren't we similar to the snobbish wine tasting event participants? We take a particular political stance, whether out of personal preference or what we might believe to be a convincing political argument that resonates with our theological position, and we do not budge, even when a reasoned discussion might validate the other side.

Whether good or bad, we often become advocates for a political or social cause because we evangelicals, of all people, would never align ourselves with something questionable. Our investment in a particular view demonstrates a certain level of commitment to ensure others understand our perspective. After all, who wants to admit that they spent $2,000 on a bottle of wine that tasted badly? As the vintner shared, those participating in the wine taste, with all the pomp and circumstance, want to save face among their peers. Whether they do this in the full knowledge of the bitter taste or blindly follow tradition is usually not as important as the appearance of an undaunted commitment to not being humiliated.

Politically, socially, even racially speaking, we become so emotionally invested in our group's position or cause that it becomes our identity. Even to our friends and colleagues, their judgment of us related to our political party or social issue impacts the way in which they interpret everything we say or do. For many Christians, we become identified more with our cultural affiliations than with Christ. The end result leads to no one listening to what we say because the message has become tainted with content that seems antithetical to the Bible. In spite of this, holding to the investment in our ideas becomes more important to us than the eternal state of those we might offend. It will take true biblical leadership to navigate this situation and courage to step boldly into an identity devoid of political and social ideologies.

LEADING DURING RACIAL TENSIONS, PLAGUES, AND POLITICAL DRAMA

If Ephesians were written to an ethnically diverse church, then we have to consider the entire letter and not just chapter 2 as relevant for ethnic relations. We might even say that the unity Paul describes in that remarkable chapter relates beyond ethnicity to theology. Perhaps we find justification to lay down our political and social ideologies here as well so that we are all united as one evangelicalism determined to fulfill God's mission on earth. So, as Paul begins the letter, not only are we all called to the same mission (ch 1), because of the work of Christ (ch 2), but we are to be one body (ch 4), imitating God (ch 5), as we advance the gospel (ch 6). Then, as cited earlier, it seems to me that Ephesians 4:32b stands as critically important: *charisomenoi eautois kathos kai o theos in christo echarisato umin.* I use the Greek here because the English simply cannot do justice to the powerful message of grace.

Charisomenoi, often mistranslated as forgiving, has far more thrust in our identity because it embodies the core of our faith, our relationships with one another, and our imitation of God. The root of the word is *charis* (grace) so *charisomenoi* should be more precisely translated as "being gracious" rather than "forgiving." It signifies an action coming from our identity rather than a tacit and often meaningless assumption of someone else's perceived guilt, or even a perception that the other should be ashamed of what they did to me, in order for them to merit my forgiveness.

Being gracious honors the act of recognizing the other in at least four ways: 1) as equally on God's mission of uniting all things in Christ, 2) in valuing the other as one for whom Christ died, 3) as seeing the other as one with me in hope, calling, and faith, and 4) in opposing the dark forces working against God's glory together as beloved brothers and sisters in Christ. Leaders in the church bear the responsibility to teach and model this graciousness and those of us in the pew assume the responsibility to enact it in our relationships with each other. This graciousness opposes the division among political and racial groups, and calls us to imitate God as beloved children (Eph 5:1) in the group Paul called His household (Eph 2:19).

***

Biblical leadership that imbibes graciousness and respect can expose situations analogous to wine tasting. It fully recognizes that our focus must be directed to God's glorification rather than the glorification of a cause or political position, even to a bottle of wine. It takes a courageous leader to recognize that the way we have always done things might not be the best way. In fact, a danger exists, I would suggest, when a leader becomes uncritical and blindly follows an ideology. Just like the wine taster, a blind allegiance or a lack of humility does not help make the wine taste any better. The potential results of a leader who blindly follows the way things were done can be devastating: witness ruined, divisions in the church, decline of Christianity. It could have been the best view at the time, but cultures change as does our understanding of the future. A commitment to the way things were done or to an ideal past or future will ensure a bad taste now and be harmful to the evangelical witness, whether admitted or not.

We have to stop assuming that those who support an opposing view regarding race or politics and the inherent systemic issues are bad people. If we cannot, we do an injustice to the gospel of Christ and we will see the death of American evangelicalism. Perhaps we are already at the grave site. It is most definitely a question we should consider.

CHAPTER 5

THE DEATH OF EVANGELICALISM?

The impeachment trial of Donald Trump riveted viewers to the television reminiscent to Richard Nixon's trail in 1973-74 and Bill Clinton's in 1993. In the midst of the Trump trail, Mark Galli, then editor of *Christianity Today*, wrote a stinging editorial that no one expected. The reaction revealed the polarization of evangelicals in the current US political climate. Some questioned his motives and others wondered what had taken so long. There were as many evangelical voices of dissent as there were of support for Galli's call for President Trump's removal from office. What we witnessed exposed a deeply divided country on every level of society: religious, cultural, racial, economic, and political. Sadly, there exists no greater division than among those who identify as "evangelicals."

In recent years, the term "evangelical" has undergone a dramatic shift in meaning. Rooted in the Greek word *euangelion*, it originally meant a political declaration that was passed from rulers to citizens. For example, Appian, a first century historian, tells about the *euangelion* that was spread concerning the arrival of Octavian's armies to help preserve the Roman republic (*The Civil Wars* 5.93).

As a common practice, Christianity borrowed secular terms that communicated principles and ideas relevant for the early church. During the New Testament period, *euangelion* took on a specific meaning of the good news proclaimed to all nations that Christ came so that whoever believed He was God would have the right to become His children and receive eternal life (John 1:12, 3:16; Rom 10:9-10). This good news continues to be declared around the world in a global announcement that God is uniting all things in Jesus Christ (Eph 1:9-10). Evangelicals, then, are those who declare this good news to others as a responsibility as they join with God on His mission to ensure that every people group on the planet has the opportunity to hear about what He has done to reconcile us to Himself (2 Cor 5:16-20).

THE SHIFTING MEANING OF EVANGELICALISM

In the early to mid 20th century, a new generation of evangelicals attempted to separate the movement from the fundamentalist Christianity we discuss in chapter 1. Making the gospel message relevant to the culture through intellectual engagement and positive messaging, this new movement became known as "neo-evangelicalism" emphasizing gospel proclamation and setting the stage for prominent pastors, teachers, and evangelists like Billy Graham and John Stott, and eventually the formation of the Lausanne Committee for World Evangelization. It was in this period of time that neo-evangelicalism became the most widely accepted and predominant voice of the conservative Christian movement broadly known as "evangelicalism."

Perhaps beginning with the Reagan presidency, the term began to take on an additional meaning. Rooted in the neo-evangelical ethos, Jerry Falwell's Moral Majority rose as a prominent "evangelical" political voice in the United States. Since that time, the term applied as much to a theological system as a political one. Unfortunately, the media and American culture grasped the now politically defined "evangelical" and turned it into something it was never intended to be, a sort of pseudo-evangelical; what I have come to call Trumpgelicalism and defined in chapter 2.

The shift in meaning of the term "evangelical" has caused some, myself included, to question the value of the word as a moniker for those of us who are passionate for the proclamation of the gospel around the world (Matt 24:14). Furthermore, as the American culture and the media continue to propagate their definition of an evangelical, supported by the actions of Trumpgelicals, the unintended consequence has increased divisions among Christians not only in the United States, but around the world as more people identify as evangelical outside of our country than inside it. The negative impact of Trumpgelicalism was recently highlighted at a meeting of evangelical, Coptic, Syriac, and Orthodox Christians in Egypt as a Palestinian evangelical shared about the persecution she suffers due to America's new religion of Trumpgelicalism.

Not only do we witness a markedly political understanding of evangelical, there exists an increasingly heretical one as well. That is, we are seeing a theological shift in the understanding of evangelical primary through the realization that evangelicals might not actually be evangelical. Consider the following set of data from a 2018 survey by Ligonier Ministries and Lifeway Research:

- 71% of those who identify as evangelicals in the US believe Jesus is a created being.
- 59% of those who identify as evangelicals in the US believe the Holy Spirit is a force and not a personal being.
- 51% of those who identify as evangelicals in the US believe that God accepts the worship of all religions.
- 35% of those who identify as evangelicals in the US believe the church needs to provide entertaining worship to be effective.
- 29% of those who identify as evangelicals in the US believe we should evangelize.

To put these data into biblical perspective, you cannot claim to be a Christian if you believe Jesus is created. Nevertheless, nearly three-quarters of evangelicals hold a fourth century heretical view of Jesus called Arianism. At some level, this might be understandable as a prominent voice among conservative evangelicals has been a neo-subordinationist view of Jesus to the Father found in some expressions of complementarianism – that doctrine which espouses the subordination of women to men based on a misinterpretation of Jesus's subordination to the Father in 1 Corinthians 11:2-16.

Similarly, to believe in the Holy Spirit as a force is to disregard the Trinitarian view of the co-equality of God the Father, God the Son, and God the Holy Spirit. Such a non-Trinitarian view was also declared a heresy in the fourth century. Again, one cannot identify as Christian with these views. In fact, the Arian view of Christ as well as the view that the Holy Spirit as a force aligns more with Jehovah's Witnesses than with evangelicalism.

While there might be some rationale to hold that God accepts the worship of all religions, when juxtaposed to the previous heretical beliefs, these evangelicals are essentially universalists and evangelicalism entertains no space for such folly. There has truly been a shift in the meaning of evangelical.

***

I believe there exists an important issue that stands as an elephant in the room, yet it is not being addressed. Perhaps it is a frightening proposition to consider. It certainly will make many Christians uncomfortable no matter if they are evangelical, neo-evangelical, Protestant, Catholic, Orthodox, Syriac, or Coptic. In my view, that issue is this: Is God being glorified through the events transpiring among evangelicals in the United States? If God is most glorified when more people are worshipping Him (Rev 5:9), how does our political and racial divisiveness help? We all need to ask ourselves this question on a personal level. In the midst of the division and the vitriolic attacks on brothers and sisters who claim belief in Jesus Christ, how are we glorifying God in our politically or racially charged statements? After all, glorifying God remains the chief end of humanity.

The events between 2016-2020 seem to indicate that we are entering a season as an evangelicalism infected with a virus that is killing the American church. Perhaps we arrived at the death of evangelicalism as we know it. Instead of the angelic proclamation that was first heard by the shepherds in the field, "Fear not, for behold, I bring you good news of great joy that will be for all the people. For unto you is born this day in the city of David a Savior, who is Christ the Lord" (Luke 2:10-11), we have become content in declaring an *euangelion* of political and racial preference; something foreign to Jesus and the angelic announcement. Perhaps this indicates that God is indeed finished with American evangelicalism.

CHAPTER 6

IS GOD FINISHED WITH AMERICAN EVANGELICALISM?

If you're on social media for any length of time, you inevitably come across a Christian marketing expert promising that he can help your church grow by using Facebook ads, websites with "plan your visit" buttons, canned sermon outlines, strategies to make your church lobby attractive, and more. Alongside of marketing, there are others who promise if you just practice the methods used in other parts of the world then the church in the US will become a movement. Countless numbers of people have learned Four Fields, T4T, Discovery Bible Studies, and other methods that apparently God blesses to catalyze more movements around the globe than we have ever witnessed in the history of humanity. Maybe they all work – marketing and ministry strategies – and we've missed a remarkable opportunity to take advantage of ideas that ensure growth.

The reality seems to be that our attempts to make disciples actually reduce the size of Christianity in the United States. In the 1990s, nearly 90 percent of the adult population identified as Christian. Today, in the Pew Research Center's most recent data, only 65 percent of US adults identify as Christian (Pew Research Center 2019). Just prior to the release of this book, Barna reported that 32 percent of practicing Christians have stopped attending church during COVID-19 (2020). Additionally, Thom Rainer, founder of Church Answers and former dean of the Billy Graham School of Missions, Evangelism, and Church Growth at Southern Baptist Theological Seminary, estimates as many as 8,000 churches will close this year.

Some look at the data and see a winnowing of the wheat from the chaff, or separating the sheep from the goats. That could certainly be the case. Others look at it and see an ineffective church that remains out of touch with culture. No doubt, there exists truth to this statement. Still, some recognize the secularization of a modern society that no longer needs the spiritual, which is plausible. Some even speculate that perhaps God has given up on American evangelicalism and is moving to the global South.

For the serious practitioner, those of us committed to the continued proclamation of the gospel (*euangelion*) in the United States and beyond, there exists a palpable tension between the on-the-ground reality and our belief in a God who desires all to be saved (1 Tim 2:4). As I look at the US religious landscape, here are four possible reactions for us to consider in response to the apparent shrinking of Christianity in our country.

- Maybe we don't know what we are doing. Could be more truth to this than we want to accept. The Bible college and seminary education, seminars, conferences, and think tanks we've all attended might confuse the whole situation and cause a paralysis of knowledge that is inept at application.

- Maybe we have so damaged God's image that people will never respond no matter what we do. Could be that people have had enough of the number of things we have done in the name of God that have contributed to institutional racism, bigotry, misogyny, and hypocrisy.

- Maybe the church is just another social club. Could be that Sunday worship services are a gathering of club volunteers who are satisfied with the communal interactions with weekend friends, and not really attentive to the fact that the majority of US adults say they are interested in having spiritual conversations.

- Maybe we don't know how to effectively communicate the gospel. This is serious. Maybe a gospel focused on repenting from sin has overshadowed a gospel focused on belief in Jesus. This gospel of repenting from sin has become more about convincing people they are bad than about a glorious God who desires to be known.

Truth be told, there might be a bit of relevance in all four of these responses to Christian regression in America. Which leads me to the question: What are we going to do about it? Seriously. Will our pontificating and theological gymnastics actually move us to think about how we can connect Jesus's story to the story of our culture? Something similar to the way in which the Apostle John so brilliantly connected Jesus with the culture of Asia Minor? I love the process he went through to share the good news of the *logos* (Word) become flesh with a culture who had anticipated the *logos* six hundred years before in the philosophy of Heraclitus of Ephesus. In his introduction to Matthew, Jerome said:

When [John] was in Asia, at the time when the seeds of heresy were springing up . . . he was urged by almost all the bishops of Asia then living, and by deputations from many Churches, to write more profoundly concerning the divinity of the Saviour, and to break through all obstacles so as to attain to the very Word of God (if I may so speak) with a boldness as successful as it appears audacious. Ecclesiastical history relates that, when he was urged by the brethren to write, he replied that he would do so if a general fast were proclaimed and all would offer up prayer to God; and when the fast was over, the narrative goes on to say, being filled with revelation, he burst into the heaven-sent Preface: "In the beginning was the Word, and the Word was with God, and the Word was God: this was in the beginning with God." (Commentary on Matthew, Preface, 2)

John's example might be calling us – evangelicals in America – to fast and pray that God will make it clear how we are to communicate the good news that exists for all people in such a way that they'll understand that Jesus is not simply the Savior of those who are coming to Christ by the thousands in other nations, but He is also the Savior of those in America waiting to hear a gospel that connects with their story. Indeed, He is the Savior of the *kosmos* (1 John 4:14) who desires us to tell His story so others can know.

Sixty-five million Christians and former Christians are done with the church in America (Packard and Hope, 2015). Another 43 million might have already left the church in 2020 (Barna, 2020). The question remains, "Is God finished with us?" It will largely depend on how we view our participation in His work. If He is not finished with us, perhaps it is time to ask the question of whether or not evangelicalism can be cured.

***

Steve Heimoff, a northern Californian wine connoisseur, writes a regular blog. Most recently, his focus on the coronavirus and politics fills his writing more than wine. In an April 2020 post in the category of comedy/satire, he voices what reads as a frustration, but should wake us up to the growing reputation of evangelicals:

One thing the evangelicals could do to hasten their trip to heaven is to cough and sneeze on each other, and be coughed and sneezed upon in return. I could imagine a huge Christian revival rally at one of those megachurches. Just set aside twenty minutes for everybody to cough and sneeze, while the choir sings and the organist pounds out "Nearer My God to Thee." Let's say you're running a fever and you have a sore throat and a lot of phlegm. You just go up to your neighbor in church, say "God bless you" and sneeze in their face, spraying as much spittle as you can. Your neighbor will then say "Thank you" and in turn go cough and sneeze on someone else. At the end of the 20 minutes (I've done the math), a congregation of 1,500 could easily infect themselves several times over. Assuming it takes anywhere from a few days to two weeks to come down with actual COVID-19 disease after exposure, I'd say that, if these evangelicals begin their work this Sunday, around 60% of them will be dead by the first week of June. ("Evangelicals, Trump, and COVID-19")

We have reached a point in the United States where our witness as evangelicals has been jeopardized by our actions. If we do not change and recover our identity as the household of God, then I'm afraid God will allow us to reap the shallow rewards we've been working toward. I hope it is not too late and I hope that our virus has not become a pandemic infecting other evangelicals. We need to fight for a cure.

CHAPTER 7

CAN EVANGELICALISM BE CURED?

From November 2019 to August 2020, the American political and racial environment opened a new opportunity for many to discuss – perhaps debate or argue – the merits of the moniker "evangelical." Not that those conversations began just then as many of us have threatened to leave evangelicalism if only we knew to whom we should write our resignation letters. There are valid reasons for such conversations as we've seen an expression of evangelicalism in America that seemingly gives more attention to the social morals and politics of our day than to making disciples of all people groups (Matt 28:18-20). So, it begs the question: can evangelicalism be cured? Might there be a sort of healing in 2020? Perhaps. However, if evangelicalism can be cured, it must recover its sense of mission: the declaration of the *euangelion*.

The path to this healing necessitates two critical elements: hermeneutics and identity. Without these two elements, I'm afraid that the evangelical church in America will never recover and will perhaps follow the path of the church of Europe. Similarly, in the absence of these two elements, I fear the evangelical church in the majority world will also follow the same path as the churches in America and Europe. Sadly, when American evangelicals sneeze, the global evangelical church catches a cold.

HERMENEUTICS AND IDENTITY

It seems the American hermeneutic – the way in which Americans interpret Scripture – focuses on ourselves. Perhaps we could say that it's an egocentric or a therapeutic hermeneutic placing American evangelicalism at the center as a God-ordained beacon of light to the world. Sunday after Sunday we listen to the moral and social, even the occasional political, platitudes from pulpits that are ostensibly out of touch with those in the pews as many feel disconnected from their pastors.

At other times, we hear messages about the "best me" or finding "my calling." A typical Sunday in the American church feels like a place where I learn about myself – what I am to do, or how I am to act, even for whom to vote. And then comes Monday and I can hardly remember what was preached from the pulpit the day before. As the sociologist Joshua Packard recently noted, those who are "done" with church and the Sunday experience, "Wanted community . . . and got judgment. They wanted to affect the life of the church . . . and got bureaucracy. They wanted conversation . . . and got doctrine. They wanted meaningful engagement with the world . . . and got moral prescription." (2015).

Other leading researchers do not paint a pretty picture of the US church either:

- Pew Research discovered that 49 percent of all Christians (38 percent of evangelicals) are only somewhat satisfied or not at all satisfied with Sunday sermons.
- Thom Rainer estimates that 6-10 thousand churches in the US closed their doors in 2018. He currently estimates 8,000 church closures in 2020.
- Lifeway Research estimates that more than half of church go-ers feel comfortable in sharing their faith but more than three-quarters haven't in the past 6 months.
- Barna Research reported that 47 percent of millennials believe it is wrong to evangelize people of other faiths.
- A Gallup poll found that only 48 percent of Christians trust the clergy, while only 25 percent of non-Christians trust the clergy.

Despite the lack of trust of clergy and dissatisfaction with their sermons, it seems the pulpit ministry takes precedence in many American evangelical churches. Pastors are trained in seminaries to believe that their weekly 45-minute soliloquy will inspire their audiences and attract people to attend church. When those inclined to attend do, we see a huge gap between Sunday and Monday that a sermon cannot fill.

To capture the attention of those who sacrifice their Sunday mornings to clothe their children and get out the door to drive to church –

I've actually heard a pastor almost equate this "sacrifice" with those living in persecuted countries – sermons tend to focus on an exposition of a book of the Bible that can take as long as three years to complete. And I should know as I once preached a series from Romans chapter 1 that took six months! Can you imagine how long it would have taken to finish the whole sixteen chapters of the epistle?! Seriously though, what more did I think could be added to the inspired Word of God?

Nevertheless, the 30-40 hours per week of sermon preparation often typifies an anthropocentric hermeneutic – one that focuses on "me" rather than God – that at times seems more about the preacher in the pulpit than the Lamb on the throne in an attempt to discover new insights for the "volunteer" to apply in their lives. It's a hermeneutic in search of a contemporary personal interpretation and often reduces the disciple of Christ to a learner in search of more knowledge, to a volunteer of an institution, or to a victim of spiritualized rhetoric. Packard writes, "It leads to the perception that Sunday mornings are far and away the most important thing the church does" (2015).

Claiming to be missional or to have a discipleship focus is betrayed by the amount of financial resources it takes to put on an hour and a half weekly event to ensure people continue to return next Sunday to give money to warrant the need for a church facility. Alan Hirsch recently shared with the Ephesiology Podcast that a church's budget represents a theological document (Ephesiology Podcast 2020).

Where the church spends its money demonstrates its priority. If the church is spending on facilities, professional staff, and volunteer programs then it has clearly lost God's vision for the extension of the *euangelion* to those who have not heard.

Granted, we have some of the most remarkable teachers in our pulpits today. Dynamic, powerful expositors who tickle the ears of Christians and occasionally produce a "disciple" fully committed to God's mission. However, if the sermons preached do not result in people becoming Christ-followers who are worshipping God and joining Him on His mission to multiply more Christ-followers, then the messages are contributing to an anthropocentric theology that institutionalizes the church. Indeed, when the majority of evangelicals believe that Jesus was created, we have a major issue in the manner in which pastors and church leaders communicate biblical truth and ensure sound doctrine (1 Tim 1:10).

A PATH FORWARD

The corrective to an anthropocentric hermeneutic focused on creating volunteers who will continue to attend Sunday mornings is a missiological hermeneutic and identity focused on God's mission to glorify Himself by more people following Him Monday through Saturday. The focus of the Bible stands on Him, not the sermon or the Sunday event. It is about the completion of His mission, not mine or the church's or the pastor's. My identity, as a result, embodies who I am in relationship to His mission, not in relationship to "some guy telling me what to do." I no longer have a choice but to be on God's mission and do the things He does (1 Cor 11:1, Luke 4:18-19).

What does this look like in the daily life of a Christ-follower? It looks like an approach to the text of Scripture through the lens of God acting as missionary. It takes the focus off of self and off of Sunday, and positions it on God who wants us to engage the people around us all seven days of the week. It takes on an identity as a myopically focused Christ-follower intent on joining with God on His missionary activity – defending the faith, visiting the sick, caring for the marginalized, clothing the naked, welcoming the immigrant, proclaiming good news to the poor and the year of the favor of the Lord – it declares the *euangelion* (Matt 25:35-40; Luke 4:18-19) and it happens more often Monday through Saturday than on Sunday. In short, God is missionary in relentless pursuit of relationships with people, and our hermeneutic should see this in all 66 books of the Bible and our identity should imitate Him in His work (Eph 5:1).

These actions result in a dynamic movement that naturally impacts race, politics, education, and economics not due to any "evangelical" agenda, but rather due to the transformed lives of those who follow Christ. This embodies what we call a missiological theocentric passion for the pursuit of God's mission of uniting all things in Christ (Eph 1:10). It imbibes a theocentric identity and hermeneutic that is perhaps a path forward to evangelicalism's cure. However, before we propose a potential treatment to restoring an evangelical identity, we'll look to three theologians for help.

***

The 1970s, 80s, and 90s saw the evangelical church grow significantly as new methods seemed to engage culture in relevant ways. As Joe Carter pointed out in The Gospel Coalition blog, the Presbyterian Church in America had grown from 41,232 members in 1973 to 367,033 in 2013. Similarly, the Evangelical Free Church of America grew from 43,851 members in 1965 to 372,321 in 2013. While these data are true, there are indicators suggesting no sustained growth over the last 10-15 years. For example, a study of the Evangelical Free Church revealed the following data:

Year	Members	Clergy	Churches	Average Church Size	Net Growth of Membership	Net Growth of Churches	Net Number of Churches per Year	Membership Growth Rate
2008	356,000	2,201	1,475	241				
2013	372,321	n.d.	1,322	282	16,321	-153	-30.6	4.58%
2016	370,001	2,319	1,321	280	-2,320	-1	-0.3	-0.62%

2018	359,240	2,426	1,344	267	-10,761	23	11.5	-2.91%

Table 9: Growth of the Evangelical Free Church of America

While we observe an increased number of clergy and churches in 2018, net growth of membership declined by more than 10,000 people. Since 2008, the EFCA has closed more than a hundred churches. So, something happened in the 70s to 90s that caused evangelicalism to begin to lose its identity. Perhaps looking at Alister McGrath, Kwame Bediako, and Thomas Oden, who were all focused on identity issues in the 1990s, will help to formulate a counter-intuitive identity for a healed evangelicalism

CHAPTER 8

RECOVERING A LOST IDENTITY

Cultural fragmentation, pluralization, and globalization have raised the issue of evangelical identity in fresh ways. These factors, along with the explosive growth of theologically conservative Protestantism worldwide as well as the impact of Trumpgelicalism and evangelical deconstructionism on the United States have prompted many to ask what it means to be "evangelical Christians." Western evangelicalism has tended to define itself in terms of the Protestant Reformation in the 16th century. As we have seen in chapter 1, there might be merit in finding a form of evangelicalism rooted in the 1st century instead.

Over the next three chapters we will take a bit of an academic turn and draw upon the works of Alister McGrath, Kwame Bediako, and Thomas Oden to discuss the strengths and weaknesses of defining evangelicalism based on a theology that emerged out of an attempt to reform the Catholic Church in Europe. In chapter 11, we will discuss the implications of formulating an "evangelical identity" based upon the Reformation. For now, we begin with Alister McGrath.

ALISTER MCGRATH

In 1995, Alister McGrath published what must now be a classic text entitled *Evangelicalism and the Future of Christianity* (Intervarsity Press) as a critique of the evangelical movement. The purpose of the book was to help the evangelical community be aware of strengths and weaknesses in the evangelical movement that has its roots in the Reformation of 1517. Motivated by the conviction that the movement has a continuing role to fulfill, McGrath hoped to open a dialogue in the worldwide community of evangelicalism.

McGrath's historical overview of the movement defines it in terms of a 16th century formative event. He believes that it remains essential for today's evangelicals to know their history in order to ensure that the same mistakes made in the past will not be repeated. Hence, through historical awareness evangelicals will have a deeper appreciation for the movement's distinctive and supposedly for the non-evangelical's attraction to it. Appealing to James I. Packer, he suggests that correct evangelical theology can only be found in the Reformation and consequently, it is this theology that will preserve evangelicalism (1995:116).

The rootedness of evangelicalism in the Reformation remains important to McGrath because of what he sees as the fragmentation of the movement. The very diversity of evangelicalism drew him to the assertion that there is a danger of losing identity and corroding doctrine. However, according to McGrath, evangelicalism embodies six overarching convictions and the holding of these convictions will ensure the preservation of evangelical identity in the midst of diversity.

1. The supreme authority of Scripture as a source of knowledge of God and a guide to Christian living.
2. The majesty of Jesus Christ, both as incarnate God and Lord, and as the Savior of sinful humanity.
3. The lordship of the Holy Spirit.
4. The need for personal conversion.
5. The priority of evangelism for both individual Christians and the church as a whole.
6. The importance of the Christian community for spiritual nourishment, fellowship and growth. (1995: 55-56)

While these six convictions are foundational to McGrath's understanding of evangelicalism, there are variations in the sundry expressions of each of these points among evangelicals (1995: 85-87). These variations occur in at least three areas. First, evangelicals differ on the emphasis of McGrath's six convictions. Some, for example, will place a greater emphasis on personal conversion rather than the lordship of the Holy Spirit. Second, the precise interpretation of the convictions relies on the traditions that evangelicals follow. For example, many European evangelicals do not hold as high a view of Scripture as do American evangelicals simply due to the fact that the American evangelical view of Scripture emerged out of the fundamentalist-modernist debates. Third, evangelicals may select additional convictions that are believed to be justified in Scripture and history as we saw in the Evangelical Free Church's initial view of premillennialism. These variations come as a result of the world-wide growth of evangelicalism and yet these variations contribute to the potential loss of identity.

McGrath's answer to the potential loss of identity rests in his statement, "The future belongs to those who can relate the heritage of the past to the realities of the present" (1995: 112). Therefore, an evangelical identity can be conserved and nourished as it rediscovers its roots and it is here that McGrath suggests the New Testament and 16th century Reformation are essential (1995: 115). But should the two be so intrinsically tied? After all, the Reformation emerged out of a particular cultural climate focused on the Catholic Church, a climate that is unknown to many evangelicals around the world and certainly unrelated to a country which celebrates religious freedom of expression. Perhaps, looking at Christianity prior to its tie to the state in 323 AD would be a better place to consider an evangelical identity. Kwame Bediako begins to move us in that direction.

EVANGELICAL IDENTITY ROOTED IN ANCIENT HISTORY

Theology attempts to answer the questions of what and why we believe as we do. In answering those questions, theology forms the basis of who we are as Christians, or, in other words, it provides a sense of identity. That identity, while being worked out for the Christian personally and theologically, expresses itself within a cultural context. Thus, the expression of Christianity in a particular context is to some degree a result of the search for a meaningful identity that relates theology to culture and culture to theology. So, let's consider Kwame Bediako and his idea of theology and identity.

KWAME BEDIAKO

The Ghanaian theologian, Kwame Bediako, sees the value of understanding Christianity's ancient history in order to address the questions of modern Christian identity. He looks at four apologists of the Christian faith in the second century AD for examples of how the early church wrestled with this very question. In his landmark 1992 book, which consisted of his doctoral dissertation, *Theology and Identity: The Impact of Culture upon Christian Thought in the Second Century and Modern Africa,* Bediako suggested that the formation of theology takes place in the cultural context of Christianity's search for self-understanding.

He proposed that Greco-Roman society initially looked at early Christianity as a superstitious sect of Judaism. As the church grew, it increasingly took on more of a Gentile identity and brought Christianity to the attention of the empire. Contrastingly, the Roman identity was deeply tied to the empire and its pagan religion including emperor worship. While Judaism was to some degree tolerated in the Roman Empire, Christianity was viewed as out of step with society and more importantly as un-Roman. Consequently, Christians in the empire were looked upon as a "third race." To Christians, however, the idea of a "third race" undermined their identity and continuity with ancient Scripture as unity in ethnic diversity was characteristic of early Christianity.

By the second century, philosophy began to replace religion as the dominate aspect of the intellectual and spiritual life of the educated. The rise to prominence of philosophy suggested the need for conversion from a "lower" standard to a "higher" standard of life. Christians, considering that the Roman religion was untrue, began to see a continuity with philosophy as it posited the need for conversion. As a result, Christians hoped to reconcile philosophy with their own teaching. The conversion idea suggested by the philosophical movement of the time gave Christianity legitimacy in its confrontation of classical paganism as a superior belief system.

Utilizing the works of Tertullian, Tatian, Justin Martyr, and Clement of Alexandria, Bediako posits that Christian self-understanding began to take form in varying degrees in relation to its discontinuity and continuity with the cultural and philosophical milieu of the time. Tertullian and Tatian provide an example of Christianity's discontinuity with Greco-Roman culture whereas Justin and Clement provide an example of its continuity.

Tertullian held that Christianity had nothing in common with the culture. His discontinuity formula contrasted the divine revelation of Christianity with the human speculative system of Greco-Roman society. This is epitomized in his aphorism, "What has Jerusalem to do with Athens, the church with the academy?" Likewise, Tatian saw Christianity's exclusivity from culture based upon the truth of Christian tradition in contrast with the inherent error of Greek philosophy. He demonstrated that Christianity's antiquity in comparison to Greek philosophy gave it its own tradition and heritage apart from the Greco-Roman culture.

Conversely, Justin was the first to attempt to find continuity between Christianity and Greco-Roman culture. He saw that since Christianity had access to the illumination of the divine Word (*logos*) it stood in the tradition of Heraclitus and Socrates' true reason. Justin believed that Socrates' true reason exposed the erroneous beliefs of

Greco-Roman religion. In his way, the conflict between truth and falsehood exemplified in Socrates' struggle with his detractors mirrored Christianity's struggle. Similarly, Clement of Alexandria understood Christianity as the fulfillment of Greek philosophy. In particular, he held that the philosophical ideas that were congruent with Christianity should be incorporated into its theology. Clement believed, due to the antiquity of Christianity, that Greek religion and philosophy was in actuality borrowing from Scripture.

Bediako suggests that the situation in contemporary Africa is not all that dissimilar to the situation of the Roman Empire in the second century; and this might even be true with the situation in the United States. The persuasiveness of his argument focuses on his distancing of African Christianity from European Christianity in search of its own identity. While he does not deny the impact of European Christianity on the African continent, he suggests that modern missionary efforts have had a Judaizing effect on African Christianity. In other words, Western Christianity replaced African Christianity with an identity unrecognizable to the second century African theologians.

For many, like Bediako, we make sense of who we are as much from what we believe as from where we are from. An evangelical identity rooted in the Reformation as McGrath suggests seems to be disconnected from the stories and places where evangelicals live all around the world, even for evangelicals in the United States. Like European Christianity did in Africa, an evangelical identity based upon the 16th century Reformation has had a Judaizing impact on the rest of evangelicalism as it has not allowed indigenous expressions of identity to emerge from the soils where Christianity has been planted.

So, perhaps focusing on a genuinely collaborative attempt by evangelicals to understand theology rooted in historical contexts and applied in contemporary cultures might prove fruitful in defining an American evangelicalism. Thomas Oden will be of particular help in this effort.

CHAPTER 10

EVANGELICAL IDENTITY ROOTED IN COLLABORATIVE THEOLOGY

In the previous two chapters on evangelical identity, we discussed Alister McGrath's *Evangelicalism and the Future of Christianity* and Kwame Bediako's *Theology and Identity*. McGrath roots his understanding of identity in the 16th century Reformation while Bediako roots his understanding of identity in 2nd century apologists. In this chapter, we look at Thomas Oden. I had the wonderful privilege of sitting under Dr. Oden's tutelage during my doctoral work. I will be forever grateful for our discussions inside and outside the classroom.

THOMAS ODEN

Thomas Oden suggests that if we are to understand Christianity's original meaning or value, we must come once again to see it through the eyes of those who have had to struggle for it and maintain it. We learn the value of classical Christianity from the martyrs, saints, and prophets of Christian history (Oden , 1992: 10). Oden proposes a paleo-orthodox theological agenda for the future of Christianity. He defines his agenda in three ways: (1) sacramentally by use of the baptismal formula, in the name of the Father, Son and Holy Spirit; (2) liturgically by the celebration of the Eucharist; (3) confessionally in consensual interpretation of the Apostles', Nicene, and Athanasian creeds (Oden, 1992).

Attempting to define orthodoxy in his agenda, Oden utilizes Vincent of Lérins' (c. 431) consensual method of interpreting Scripture. Vincent became known for his rule for determining orthodoxy, which bears his name: the Vincentian Canon. It is summarized as *teneamus quod ubique, quod semper, quod ab omnibus creditum est.* In utilizing the Vincentian Canon, Oden suggests that Christianity must recover the memory as defended by the Apostolic Fathers and defined by the Church Fathers during the first seven ecumenical councils. It must recover the apostolic consensus that "repeatedly challenged and transformed emerging modernities" (Oden, 1992: 163).

In his consensual approach, Oden asserts that theology should not be looked at narrowly, but rather with boundaries. In fact, he believes that the rediscovery of boundaries will be the primary occupation of twenty-first century theology (Oden, 1996: 13). Theological reflection is best conducted in the context of boundaries. Those boundaries were initially set in the first five centuries of Christian history by the doctors of the church. To understand them is to understand the boundaries of consensual theology that was accepted by East and West.

Defining the boundaries of consensual theology remains challenging. In the early church, heresy played a significant role in determining those boundaries of orthodox theology. Theological issues, when taken to extreme, molded an understanding of what is or is not correct Apostolic Tradition that was believed everywhere by all, i.e., Vincent's canon. Etymologically, heresy finds its origin in the idea of an assertive self-will. Heresy evolved from personal theological biases and offered the occasion to help define orthodoxy by what it is not. The early church ensured apostolic continuity in the context of heresies that were influenced by diverse cultural presuppositions (Oden: 1996, 12-13). Therefore, an assertion might be made that the early church attempted to anchor its theology in the Apostolic Tradition and propagated orthodoxy that was both contextual and transcultural by nature.

But what seems apparently absent from Oden's agenda is a missiological avenue for engaging culture. His agenda remains primarily focused on recovering orthodox Christianity that was lost during the rise of modernity with the prominence of Protestant liberalism, historical criticism, and neo-orthodoxy. In spite of this, certain segments of evangelicalism express a growing interest to return to classical Christianity as outlined by Oden's call to the "consensual" tradition of the first millennium (Nassif, 1998: 109).

In the next chapter, we'll begin to think about the implications, if not influence, of McGrath, Bediako, and Oden on formulating an evangelical identity for the 21st century.

EVANGELICAL IDENTITY ROOTED IN MISSIOLOGY

We wrapped up this three-chapter discussion by considering the strengths and weaknesses of building an evangelical identity on a 16th century theology alone, McGrath's position and one that has influenced contemporary evangelicalism especially in America.

STRENGTHS OF AN EVANGELICAL IDENTITY BASED ON THE REFORMATINO

As might be assumed based on the discussion in chapter 8, McGrath saw the strength of evangelicalism in its appeal to non-evangelicals. That appeal results from several factors which would no doubt be contested in today's cultural climate as it becomes increasingly clear that the American evangelical church has lost its voice. Nevertheless, McGrath argues that the attraction to evangelicalism is due to five factors:

1. Failure of liberal Christianity.
2. Evangelicalism is historically orthodox Christianity.

3. Intellectual attraction to evangelicalism because it makes sense.
4. The attraction of the gospel.
5. Diversity of the evangelical church.

Bediako might suggest that evangelicalism's missionary zeal stands as a strength. Granted, it took about 200 years before the missionary fervor of European Reformation Christians ignited, the nascent form of contemporary evangelicalism. Nonetheless, evangelicalism derives its name from its focus upon the gospel ministry.

The *solas* (*fides, gratia, scriptura*) of the Reformation would also be considered strengths. These ideas offered correctives for the Catholic Church and distinguished the reformers from their detractors. The priesthood of the believers, as well, gave the reformers and those who followed the idea of personal obligation to God with personal responsibility in the ministry. In addition, the reformers confronted the culture of the day and challenged the practice of Christianizing pagan rituals.

In regards to the reformers challenge of culture, according to Van Rooy (1985), Calvin saw both a continuity and discontinuity in Christianity's relationship to culture. Calvin's interpretation of Romans 1 suggests that he saw a sense of deity in human minds as well as natural instinct. At the same time, Calvin believed that there was a gulf between what God revealed in nature and what He revealed in His Word.

WEAKNESSES OF AN EVANGELICAL IDENTITY BASED ON THE REFORMATION

Even in the 1990s, McGrath contemplated whether or not evangelicalism had lost its identity. He regards the impact of diversity in the movement as a potential weakness. Its diversity highlights the fact that evangelicalism stands at a crossroad of an identity crisis and this has certainly been exacerbated in the 2020s with a series of crises in politics, plagues, race, and religion. That diversity has led evangelicalism to privatization and the explosion of 45,000 denominations and organizations. Due in part to the Enlightenment project and what the German sociologist, Max Weber, called the Protestant ethic, religion was taken out of the public realm. Faith became personal and private rather than corporate and public.

McGrath goes on to state that the identity of evangelicalism remains tied up in the West which makes it difficult to contextualize the Christian message in other cultures. He duly notes the tendency of evangelicals to insist on its traditions without regard to culture. This was played out on many occasions as evangelicalism spread from continent to continent often associated with the interests of the sending country. In a sense, Bediako's response to this weakness derives from an African Christian identity based upon the second century apologists who sought a unique Christian self-understanding.

McGrath identifies the evangelical struggle for the meaning of spirituality as another weakness and reinforces the need for evangelicals to understand their heritage. Evangelicalism has tended to rely upon the current trends of Eastern thought in order to find a suitable understanding of spirituality. One might think of the prevalence of Yoga or Buddhist mediation practices in some American evangelical churches. While focusing attention towards the East, evangelicalism has negated its own heritage and has failed to handle the modern situation adequately.

Yet, the evangelical identity proposed by McGrath is only five hundred years old. The issue confronting most continents as a result of the inability of evangelicalism to separate itself from the West, and in particular from modernity, presents the exact issue confronting evangelical identity: Europe searches for an identity in pre-Christian religions; Africa searches for identity in African Traditional Religions; Latin America searches for identity in native religions; and the United States searches for an identity in political parties and social causes.

The weakness of the evangelical identity based upon the Reformation lies in its discontinuity with the rest of Christian history as suggested by Oden. The assertion that evangelicalism remains tied to the Reformation suggests that all evangelicals everywhere should share the same convictions. This assertion simply cannot be supported since the Reformation was a response to the context of its time. Simply rooting evangelicalism in the Reformation negates the fact that evangelicals share the same 2,000 year history with the rest of global Christianity.

MISSIOLOGICAL IMPLICATIONS

As previously mentioned, the question that many people are asking around the world remains the one of identity. The globalization that has resulted from the technological advancements of modernity has in one sense brought the world closer. However, in another sense it has caused people to lose a sense of connectedness with their cultures. The response has been a revitalization of the past. Oden and Bediako have picked up on this and are suggesting that Christians should look more seriously at their past as well.

McGrath believes that evangelicalism's loss of identity stands tied to a lack of historical understanding of the Reformation. He feels that a rediscovery of the roots of evangelicalism remains key to the conservation of the movement. He reminds evangelicals that *ecclesia reformta, ecclesia semper reformanda* remains important for this conservation. This being the case, evangelicalism should find its lost identity not only in the Reformation, but also in the history of world Christianity, including early church history.

There is little doubt that evangelicalism has been attracted to modernity and that modernity has contributed to the rapid growth of evangelicalism. As evangelicalism has spread throughout the world it has encountered cultures that are extraordinarily different than the West. And yet as many have pointed out, the evangelical church in the world reflects the evangelicalism of the West. While Western evangelicals insist that their expression of Christianity embodies the Bible, there must also be an acknowledgement that the form of the expression is embedded in Western culture; the flu that the world has caught from American evangelicalism in particular.

This acknowledgement becomes increasingly important since Western evangelicalism continues to dominate the mission world. In spite of the fact that Christianity is on the decline in general and evangelicalism in the West is not experiencing dramatic growth, Europe sends more missionaries than any other continent and the United States more than any single country. Yet, the majority of Christians and evangelicals are located in the non-Western world. Therefore, there exists a tremendous need for Western evangelicals to allow evangelicalism to find its own expression in the countries where it has reached and not risk the propagation of an American evangelicalism that is constrained by our particular cultural issues. Not all evangelical Christians have experienced the cultural context which gave birth to the Reformation, and its unique expression of the faith; nor have they experience the American cultural context.

As indigenous Christians are increasingly disappointed with the Western expression of Christianity they are finding new ways to express their Christianity and to make it relevant for their contexts. What all this means missiologically is that evangelicalism might be experiencing a world-wide reformation, perhaps what might be called a counter-intuitive reformation. American evangelicalism must not get in the way of these cultural expressions. Instead, American evangelicals should take a learning posture as indigenous Christians find new ways to express a meaningful understanding of the *euangelion*. Perhaps we will learn from them and see a revitalization of American evangelicalism, and rediscover our identity rooted in God's missionary heart.

Christianity, and evangelicalism specifically, must be as diverse as the people it attempts to reach. Given the diversity of the world, evangelicalism must rediscover its unique answer to ethnic and racial, even political groups. What we need is a model of evangelicalism that engages identity on every level, not in order to conform the diverse identities of people to a set of religious doctrines of a culture, but understanding how the very diversity of people from different backgrounds leads to a more complete picture of humanity's relationship to its Creator and His household.

Bediako suggests that there are similarities between the second century cultural context and modern Africa. I would contend that there are similarities with other modern contexts as well; namely that Christianity is being worked out within specific cultural contexts with unique cultural expressions of the faith once passed down. The Reformation is but one expression of how Christianity was worked out in Western Europe 500 years ago. We should fully expect to see different expressions of Christianity in different cultures as well as in different eras, even in the United States.

Each generation shares the responsibility to ensure the relevancy of the one true faith. This is a relevancy that respects its past, is faithful to sound teaching, and engages in three areas of ministry. So, we conclude our journey attempting to understand the challenges we face with a meager proposal to heal American evangelicalism.

***

During the course of my research, I came across many comments about evangelicals. Some of them were from evangelicals in other parts of the world talking about American evangelicals. Some were evangelical Democrats talking about evangelical Republicans and vice versa. Others were from non-evangelicals, even people from other faiths, talking about American evangelicals. What seemed apparent from all types of comments was American evangelicals have acted in such a way that people around the world do not understand what an American evangelical is. Sometimes I wonder the same. I even wonder if the manner in which we have talked about each other has created stumbling blocks to people hearing the story about Jesus.

If there is one thing I have learned over more than 30 years of cultural engagement, it is that belief in Jesus Christ should be the only stumbling block to a person coming to faith (1 Cor 8:9). This was very apparent regarding the witness of the early missionaries in Ephesus. At a crucial moment in ministry, the town clerk spoke up, "Men of Ephesus, who is there who does not know that the city of the Ephesians is temple keeper of the great Artemis, and of the sacred stone that fell from the sky? Seeing then that these things cannot be denied, you ought to be quiet and do nothing rash. For you have brought these men here who are neither sacrilegious nor blasphemers of our goddess" (Acts 19:35-37).

The important lesson we learn from these missionaries is that we do not allow our prejudgments to impact our witness for the gospel. We might not agree with someone's religious views or political views, even their perception of the pandemic. But those things should never become a stumbling block to another person coming to Christ. Unfortunately, in the United States, that is not the case. American evangelicals seem to make all sorts of things, except Jesus, stumbling blocks and it has affected our witness. Recovering a missiological group identity founded on God's missionary nature and relentless pursuit of people may be a step in the right direction to a counter-intuitive reformation.

CHAPTER 12

HEALING EVANGELICALISM: A VIRUS WORTH SPREADING

If you are in ministry or church leadership, I'm sure you will occasionally receive an email or see something come across your social media about a ministry job: children's pastor, worship pastor, church secretary or facilities manager for example. If you regularly attend church, you have no doubt heard the need for volunteers: musicians, nursery workers, parking attendants, greeters, clean up, lawn care, etc. On occasion, volunteers are needed to lead Bible studies or Sunday School classes, perhaps even to teach children's church; however, there are professionals to do these things, especially in larger churches.

As I scour the Bible, to be blunt, I cannot find any of these ministries or volunteer positions. And to be perfectly honest, I don't even see Bible study leaders as a ministry of the church. Sure, I can provide a rationale for the need of these positions and I'm not saying that they are unbiblical. Rather, they are extra biblical. To argue otherwise simply imposes denominational, cultural, or theological preference on the Bible and these often become distractions to the mission of the church.

In all seriousness, I can put the Bible through all kinds of gymnastics to conclude many things that were not originally intended. After all, that is how we've arrived at more than 45,000 different evangelical denominations and organizations. Yet, in regards to ministries, culture – whether denominational culture or theological culture – has more often demanded their formation rather than Christ. When He said, "I will build my church" (Matt 16:17), I am absolutely positive that He did not envision construction projects, or building campaigns, nor did He intend for discipleship or ministry to be outsourced to professionals or volunteers.

At the beginning of the book, I posited that there are three areas of ministry that mark the identity of a New Testament church; indeed, even an evangelical church. We see them clearly in Jesus's teaching on the Great Commandment (Matt 22:37-38), Great Compassion (Matt 25:31-40), and Great Commission (Matt 28:18-20). We see them again in Jesus's letter to the church at Ephesus (Rev 2:1-7). We even see them in Paul's instructions to Timothy. His first epistle, a stream of consciousness as Paul gave Timothy instructions about the focus of ministry, follows a very simple outline of ensuring sound teaching (1 Tim 1:3-7), gospel proclamation (1 Tim 1:12-2:7), and social justice (1 Tim 2:8-15); themes he repeats throughout the rest of the letter.

This ministry focus exemplifies the essence of a counter-intuitive reformation marked by a core set of beliefs, a common set of behaviors, and a community of belonging so distinct from any other religious expression that its very presence in a society draws people's attention to Jesus Christ. Just as we see in Jesus and Paul, a counter-intuitive reformation defends our teaching about the one true God (Matt 22:37-38; 1 Tim 1:3-7), engages in contemporary social issues as it stands in the gap for the marginalized and exploited (Matt 25:31-40; 1 Tim 2:8-15), and marches on toward the completion of God's mission of more and more people following Jesus (Matt 28:18-20; 1 Tim 1:12-2:7).

So, in this chapter, I'll unpack these three areas of ministry as taught by Jesus and Paul. Outside of these three areas, the church begins to lose her identity. An overemphasis on any of these areas at the expense of the others also leads to a loss of identity. The identity of an evangelical maintains a solidly biblical defense of the faith, it passionately engages culture in acts of social justice, and it lovingly gathers in a community celebrating its allegiance to Christ alone as it proclaims the glory of God to the nations.

DEFENSE OF THE FAITH

The Ephesus of the first century must have been a fascinating place, if not from cultural and philosophical perspectives, certainly from a Christian one. Luke tells us that every resident of the city heard the word of the Lord (Acts 19:10, 20). However, early in the ministry at Ephesus, there were signs of the potential for syncretism. Syncretism simply merges two or more distinct ideas or beliefs in such a way that it is difficult to distinguish them from each other. They, in essence, become a new belief system or ideology. In Ephesus, the first hint of syncretism occurs with the Jewish missionaries attempting to exorcise a demon (Acts 19:13-16). They combined their Jewish beliefs with Christian actions only to be left naked and fleeing in fear.

We do not know all the falsehoods being taught in the church in Ephesus. Paul hints to the fact that false teachers had emerged in the city and were carrying away the weak (1 Tim 4:1-5). Apparently it became such an issue that Paul declares all in Asia had left him (2 Tim 1:15). No doubt there were Judaizers as they seemed to be the perennial problem for early Christianity. Those Jewish Christians who demanded a syncretism between Jewish religious traditions and the new Jesus tradition became the focus of Paul's epistle to the Galatians and potentially John's nemesis in his letters. Whatever the false teaching, the believers in Ephesus successfully combated it and received a commendation from Jesus Himself (Rev 2:2).

What strikes our interest in the church in Ephesus is the fact that this false teaching emerges out of the context of a Christianity untethered from sound doctrine. It came from within and the church successfully defended against it with the end result of her unprecedented growth and lasting legacy of theological correctness.

According to the apostle Peter who also addressed the church in Ephesus as well as the other churches in Asia Minor, we have to assume that an aspect of the successful defense of the faith came in the manner in which the church engaged those of differing beliefs. Peter writes,

> *Now who is there to harm you if you are zealous for what is good? But even if you should suffer for righteousness' sake, you will be blessed. Have no fear of them, nor be troubled, but in your hearts honor Christ the Lord as holy, always being prepared to make a defense to anyone who asks you for a reason for the hope that is in you; yet do it with gentleness and respect, having a good conscience, so that, when you are slandered, those who revile your good behavior in Christ may be put to shame. For it is better to suffer for doing good, if that should be God's will, than for doing evil. (1 Peter 3: 13-17)*

For years I taught an introduction to the New Testament in the now discontinued School of Biblical and Religious Studies at a university in Deerfield, Illinois. Each new year, a fresh crop of eager students came mostly ready to test their knowledge of the Bible. They came from various backgrounds, but the overwhelming majority were from evangelical churches. As I introduced the course to the students on the first day, I always communicated that the average grade on the first exam had traditionally been failing largely due to the fact that students believed they grasped the New Testament since they had grown up in the church. I'm not certain if it were due to syllabus shock on the first day of class or simply intellectual pride, but without fail it always happened. The class average on the first exam typically ranged from 48-52 percent. It stunned students and woke them up to the fact that they really did not know Christianity as they should. Thankfully, by the end of the semester, nearly every student recovered from that first exam to the typical final class average ranging around 80-90 percent.

There is something going on in our churches today that must be addressed. Earlier I mentioned the data from a survey conducted in 2018 and it merits re-iterating them here:

- 71% of those who identify as evangelicals in the US believe Jesus is a created being.
- 59% of those who identify as evangelicals in the US believe the Holy Spirit is a force and not a personal being.
- 51% of those who identify as evangelicals in the US believe that God accepts the worship of all religions.
- 35% of those who identify as evangelicals in the US believe the church needs to provide entertaining worship to be effective.
- 29% of those who identify as evangelicals in the US believe we should evangelize.

For only 29 percent of evangelicals to believe that Jesus is not created means that whatever the leaders of our churches teach is not being taught effectively or heresy is being taught from pulpits and Bible studies. Either our pastors, Sunday School teachers, and small group leaders did not learn simple doctrinal truth from seminary or their own personal study, or they are utterly ineffectual in communicating that truth to others. Whatever the case, the evangelical church has a serious need to defend the faith to its own people. If we cannot get this straightened out, we are a part of the problem in the evangelical loss of identity. Paul says,

> *I charge you in the presence of God and of Christ Jesus, who is to judge the living and the dead, and by his appearing and his kingdom: preach the word; be ready in season and out of season; reprove, rebuke, and exhort, with complete patience and teaching. For the time is coming when people will not endure sound teaching, but having itching ears they will accumulate for themselves teachers to suit their own passions, and will turn away from listening to the truth and wander off into myths. As for you, always be sober-minded, endure suffering, do the work of an evangelist, fulfill your ministry. (2 Tim 4:1-5)*

The time has indeed come when evangelicals no longer endure sound teaching. Once again, if we do not get this right, evangelicalism in America will soon die. It falls squarely on the shoulders of those of us who consider ourselves leaders in the church. This is not the time to squabble about the people filling our pews and their lack of inattentiveness. We are responsible to teach correct doctrine and we need to figure out how to teach it effectively because whatever we are doing now is simply not working.

In many ways, I am a pragmatic person. If I see something not working, I'll change. If I were to continue to do the same things and expect different results, then I would indeed be insane as the saying goes. The evangelical church in America stands stuck in a rut and it has produced heretical evangelicals, truly people in doctrinal error, and sadly people who have a false sense of salvation. Change to the manner in which we teach God's truth must happen. Rather than defending our political views, we must defend the faith. I suggested a path forward in chapter 7.

SOCIAL JUSTICE

Not only did Jesus commend the church in Ephesus for successfully warding off the false apostles, He commends the church for standing against the work of the Nicolaitans (Rev 2:6). We know very little about their work and what we know comes from the second-third century early church apologist, Irenaeus. In *Against Heresies*, he writes that the Nicolaitans were followers of the so-called deacon named Nicolas in Acts 6. According to Irenaeus, Nicolas desired to demonstrate his commitment to Christ by abstaining from sexual relations with his wife. To further demonstrate his seriousness, he permitted others to have sexual relations with her.

Little evidence exists concerning a sect called Nicolaitans being present in Ephesus. Nonetheless, there was an apparent correlation with what John saw as the marginalization of women in that city. We know from ancient sources as well as biblical sources that women were being exploited by men in many ways that include sexual favors.

This form of exploitation was not tolerated by the church in Ephesus and Jesus applauds their efforts to stand up for the dignity of these women (Cooper, 2020: 167-168).

This doesn't escape Paul either as he moves to protect women from exploitation in 1 Tim 2:7-15. Truly one of the most misunderstood passages of the Pauline corpus, the apostle simply communicates about a particular cultural practice in Ephesus which placed scantily dressed women at the intellectual center of symposia where men gathered, often disrobed, for entertainment. Such action did not represent Christian women or men. Thus, as a warning for both, Paul states, "I do not permit a woman to teach or to exercise authority over a man; rather, she is to remain quiet" (1 Tim 2:12). The gathering of the church had to be distinct from the assembly of female courtesans for male erotic fantasies.

It was not only the exploitation of women that concerned Paul and others, but also the care for the marginalized. Well before his arrival at Ephesus in 51 AD, Paul wrote to the Galatians that the leaders in Jerusalem implored him not to forget the poor to which he responded, "the very thing I was eager to do" (Gal 2:10). Paul was deeply concerned for the social well-being of the vulnerable as was Jesus. So, if Jesus and Paul were, then the evangelical church must also be concerned and eager to stand in the gap of social injustice.

Up until 2015, the United Nations published an update on its Millennium Development Goals (MDG). This update framed part of the focus of a Master of Arts in Cultural Engagement degree that sadly came to an end in 2012. Naturally, I was bias toward the degree and proud of the fact that an evangelical university would prepare young minds to engage in social issues. However, at the end of the day, the effort to train future leaders to effectively engage culture by a careful and deliberate focus on the most pressing issues of our day did not meet the financial expectations of the dean and president at the time.

The Millennium Development Goals sunsetted in 2015, but continue to inform ongoing efforts to end poverty in the United Nations' Sustainability Goals. Focused in eight areas of greatest need, MDG intended to:

1. Eradicate extreme poverty and hunger.
2. Achieve universal primary education.
3. Promote gender equality and empower women.
4. Reduce child mortality.
5. Improve maternal health.
6. Combat HIV/AIDS, Malaria, and other diseases.
7. Ensure environmental sustainability.
8. Global partnership for development.

The needs around the world continue to be great and are most definitely exacerbated now due to the COVID-19 pandemic. A number that will no doubt increase, in 2015 more than 10 percent of the global population lived on less than $1.25 per day. The same number of people was estimated to be undernourished. Extreme poverty inhibits access to healthcare and education, and stands as a leading cause for the ongoing plight of women and children trafficked in the sex industry. Today, there are more slaves in the world, both sexual and forced labor, than there ever have been in the history of humanity. In addition, there are nearly 80 million refugees, whether internally displaced or those who have fled their homelands; more than ever before. These are areas that afford the evangelical church an opportunity, if not a responsibility, to stand in the gap for those who are in desperate need.

There are social justice issues in our country as well, and evangelicals should be the first to stand in this gap. There are voices that have not been heard, and Jesus calls us to listen and hear. Racial and immigration tensions, food inequality, educational and healthcare disparities are taking an unprecedented toll on the fabric of American society. Who better to address these issues than an evangelical church with a mandate from Jesus Himself, "And the King will answer them, 'Truly, I say to you, as you did it to one of the least of these my brothers, you did it to me'" (Matt 25:40).

I am concerned that due to a lack of involvement by the evangelical church and evangelical universities in social issues, particularly those in the United States, there have been tendencies of socially aware evangelicals to align with organizations and movements which do not hold biblical values. For example, the 501c3 non-profit organization Black Lives Matter Foundation, Inc. has a clear political and social agenda antithetical to Christianity. Yaron Steinbuch reported in a *New York Post* article that Patrisse Cullors, co-founder with Alicia Garza and Opal Tometi, acknowledged that she and her colleagues were "trained Marxists." Citing a video interview with Jared Ball of The Real News Network in 2015, Cullors states, "We are trained Marxists. We are super-versed on, sort of, ideological theories." (Steinbuch, 2020).

The "About" page of their website provides a clear statement of their purpose:

We are self-reflexive and do the work required to dismantle cisgender privilege and uplift Black trans folk, especially Black trans women who continue to be disproportionately impacted by trans-antagonistic violence.

(http://blacklivesmatter.com/about)

In addition, the organization's agenda includes among other things:

- Celebration of unbiblical sexual identity and gender expressions.
- Preference for transgender leadership.
- Devaluing the nuclear family.
- Fostering a "queer-affirming" network.

While much can be appreciated about the organization such as their call to be "seen, heard, and supported," and the ideal that not only do "black lives matter," but "all lives matter," evangelicals must be aware of the danger of uncritically following a movement whose core subverts biblical values.

The time where evangelicals can ignore issues of social justice has long past. It is important to recover this identity and work toward a collective evangelical voice in these tumultuous times (Bhatia and Cooper, forthcoming). A starting place might be to find consensus in the Lausanne Covenant's statement on social responsibility:

We affirm that God is both the Creator and the Judge of all people. We therefore should share his concern for justice and reconciliation throughout human society and for the liberation of men and women from every kind of oppression. Because men and women are made in the image of God, every person, regardless of race, religion, colour, culture, class, sex or age, has an intrinsic dignity because of which he or she should be respected and served, not exploited. Here too we express penitence both for our neglect and for having sometimes regarded evangelism and social concern as mutually exclusive. Although reconciliation with other people is not reconciliation with God, nor is social action evangelism, nor is political liberation salvation, nevertheless we affirm that evangelism and socio-political involvement are both part of our Christian duty. For both are necessary expressions of our doctrines of God and man, our love for our neighbour and our obedience to Jesus Christ. The message of salvation implies also a message of judgment upon every form of alienation, oppression and discrimination, and we should not be afraid to denounce evil and injustice wherever they exist. When people receive Christ they are born again into his kingdom and must seek not only to exhibit but also to spread its righteousness in the midst of an unrighteous world. The salvation we claim should be transforming us in the totality of our personal and social responsibilities. Faith without works is dead.

GOSPEL PROCLAMATION

Jesus commends the church in Ephesus for her defense of the faith and her stand for social justice. Yet, He had one thing against her. He writes,

But I have this against you, that you have abandoned the love you had at first. Remember therefore from where you have fallen; repent, and do the works you did at first. If not, I will come to you and remove your lampstand from its place, unless you repent. (Rev 2:4-5)

I can just hear the church saying something like, "Yes, but Jesus, look at how we defended the faith against the liberal politicians. And what about how we have given money to the poor and work toward racial reconciliation? Don't you remember Promise Keepers and the Moral Majority? Do not those things show you that we love you?" I suspect Jesus would smile then sternly say, "but you have still forgotten your first love."

This first love is a work. Perhaps multiple types of works to correspond to the purpose of Revelation – the declaration of the completion of God's mission to see every nation, tribe, language, and authority bow before the throne in worship of the One who is worthy.

There is nothing complicated about this. And there is really not much more that can be said. The declaration of God's glory was primary in Jesus's love for the Father and must be primary to American evangelicalism,

And this is eternal life, that they know you, the only true God, and Jesus Christ whom you have sent. I glorified you on earth, having accomplished the work that you gave me to do. And now, Father, glorify me in your own presence with the glory that I had with you before the world existed. (John 17:3-4)

It was also the first love of Paul and the foundation of a theology commensurate with the Ephesian movement,

When you read this, you can perceive my insight into the mystery of Christ, which was not made known to the sons of men in other generations as it has now been revealed to his holy apostles and prophets by the Spirit. This mystery is that the Gentiles are fellow heirs, members of the same body, and partakers of the promise in Christ Jesus through the gospel. Of this gospel I was made a minister [lit. deacon] according to the gift of God's grace, which was given me by the working of his power. To me, though I am the very least of all the saints, this grace was given, to preach to the Gentiles the unsearchable riches of Christ, and to bring to light for everyone what is the plan of the mystery hidden for ages in God, who created all things, so that through the church the manifold wisdom of God might now be made known to the rulers and authorities in the heavenly places. This was according to the eternal purpose that he has realized in Christ Jesus our Lord. (Eph 3:4-11)

And so, I put forward this idea for you to consider. These three areas of ministry – defense of the faith, social justice, gospel proclamation – mark the identity of the evangelical church and are necessary to restore our witness in America. Her defense of the faith marks her beliefs in the one true God and Savior of all humanity. Her engagement in social justice marks a behavior with the conviction that when she does these things she does them to Christ Himself. Finally, her declaration of God's glory to the nations marks her unity with all evangelicals to a common mission so compelling that it brings others into the community of Christ followers.

***

As I alluded earlier, in early November 2019, I sat in a room of Christians comprised of various traditions: Coptic, Orthodox, Syriac, Catholic, and evangelical. The location did not escape my attention as the group of about 50 members of the Lausanne Orthodox Initiative, an issue group of the Lausanne Committee for World Evangelization, a movement started in 1974 in Lausanne, Switzerland by Billy Graham and John Stott, discussed the meaning of working together for progress in the gospel at the monastery of Saint Bishoy. Saint Bishoy lived in the late fourth century and became known as one of the so-called desert-fathers.

As our group shared that afternoon around the conference table, a brave Palestinian evangelical raised an issue that was certainly on everyone's minds, but no one would willingly admit, until she exposed the problem with American evangelicalism. In essence she testified to the difficulty she and other Palestinian evangelicals experience in communicating the gospel when evangelicals have been stigmatized with the political policies and morality of Donald Trump. She is not the only non-American evangelical who has felt this tension. As I have travelled around the world and continue relationships with dear evangelical friends now through electronic means, I hear similar stories. But in Egypt, that was the last straw.

I sat next to Doug Birdsall during that session. As the former executive chairman of the Lausanne Committee for World Evangelization, I thought he would be the closest thing to an evangelical pope. So, I turned to him and announced my verbal resignation from evangelicalism. If being evangelical means that I am stigmatized by the actions of a politician, rather than the work of Jesus Christ, then I wanted nothing to do with it. I was done. Heartbroken and shaken to my core.

Well, it's been a long seven months since that meeting. Mark Galli wrote a blistering review of the president later in December 2019. The novel coronavirus pandemic has resulted in more deaths in the United States than any place in the world. Racial tensions have never been as acute as they are now. And to top it off, Robert Jeffress announced to a packed congregation at First Baptist Church in Dallas,

Texas on June 28, 2020, at an event called "Freedom Sunday," that he predicts a record number of evangelicals will vote for Trump later in November.

In many ways, the current political, racial, and health climate of the United States has exposed numerous issues within evangelicalism's loss of identity. The tensions we feel racially and politically, in combination with the ongoing stress and anxiety created by a plague can only be addressed as evangelicals restore their identity grounded in a counter-intuitive reformation found in the first century. I've attempted to lay out what that might look like.

I believe strongly that the evangelical church today must become like the churches of the first century. So, the evangelical church must stand on the side of social justice. She must also defend the faith. And she must never waiver from declaring God's glory so that every people, tribe, language, and nation will one day be represented at the throne of God. The very heart of the evangelical church encourages her members to stay on God's mission as we unite as one body of Christ to glorify God.

In as much as the evangelical church will make this her focus, and I believe it's possible, I rescind my resignation from evangelicalism and pledge to do what I can to restore our identity in a biblically grounded, socially just, gospel proclaiming community of Christ followers passionate to see God's glory and Christ's fame declared around the world. If this is the virus we are spreading, then I will gladly sneeze.

HOW WILL YOU DECIDE?

If you were hoping that by reading this book you'd have a better idea about how to vote, then I've accomplished one of my goals. If you were hoping I'd tell you who to vote for, then you will be sorely disappointed. To be perfectly honest, as of the publication of this book, I am still undecided. In fact, I continue to wrestle with the issue of my responsibility as a Christian vis-à-vis my responsibility as an American citizen.

If there were a governing principle that I apply in deciding which candidate deserves my vote, it would be related to the mission of the church. So, I ask the two following questions:

1. Which candidate will create a peaceful environment in which the gospel can continue to spread in the United States?
2. Which candidate will provide the best opportunity to ensure security for the worldwide spread of the gospel?

I hope these questions will help you as you navigate the 2020 election.

THIS IS ETERNAL LIFE

Do you wonder what will happen when you die? Perhaps you ask questions like: "Will I simply be put in a box and buried six feet underground waiting for my body to decay?" "Will I even be aware of what is happening?" Or, "will I be conscience of things going on around me?" "Will I actually go somewhere else?" Challenging questions for sure.

Death can be a fearful thing. Paralyzing really. If we were to dwell on it too long, we might find ourselves saddened about the loved ones we will miss or the dreams left unfulfilled. Many of us choose not even to think about it and when we do, we hope that we die suddenly or peacefully so we will not feel pain. But, one thing is inevitable: we will someday die. So, what comes next?

Many religions promise some type of future. Hinduism promises a cycle of birth and rebirth based upon your Karma that eventually leads to a state of nothingness. Buddhism promises enlightenment if we might rid ourselves of all desire – for personal well-being, for friendship, for love, etc. – the root of suffering. Islam promises a future for faithful men with the women of paradise if it is Allah's will.

Jesus Christ promised something unlike Hinduism, Buddhism, or Islam. His promise for eternal life and requires only one thing. In one of the most recognizable verses of the Bible, Jesus said, "For God so loved the world, that he gave his only Son, that whoever believes in him should not perish, but have eternal life" (John 3:16). Eternal life is something we do not deserve. We cannot earn it. But, it is not just going to happen either. Jesus said, "And this is eternal life, that they know you, the only true God, and Jesus Christ whom you have sent" (John 17:3).

Believing in Jesus and knowing God is not simply an intellectual act, but also a behavioral one. He wants our lives to reflect God's glory as His children (John 1:12-13). So, when we believe in Him, it changes us. And, what we believe about Him is important. Here are a few things Jesus said about Himself:

- He is the bread of life who sustains life (John 6:30-59)
- He is the light of the world (John 8:12-17)
- He is the "I am," who has been from the beginning (John 8:58)
- He is the door of the sheep providing security (John 10:7-9)
- He is the good shepherd who gave his life for the sheep and cares for his flock (John 10:11-18)
- He and the Father are one (John 10:30)
- He is the resurrection and the life who ensures us of the future (John 11:25)

- He is the way, the truth, and the life for everyone who believes including those from Hindu, Buddhist, and Muslim backgrounds (John 14:6)
- He is the true vine who provides joy to all who abide in him (John 15:1)

If you believe in Jesus and this is the eternal life you desire, simply ask God for it. You can speak with Him using your own words. He wants you to have eternal life. Jesus said, "For this is the will of my Father, that everyone who looks on the Son and believes in him should have eternal life, and I will raise him up on the last day" (John 6:40).

If you would like to learn more about Jesus and eternal life, please contact us at info@ephesiology.com. We would love to share about the hope of eternal life.

REFERENCE LIST

Banks, Adelle. 2018. "President Trump's Evangelical Advisory Board." *National Catholic Reporter* . Internet resource available from https://www.ncronline.org/news/politics/key-evangelical-players-trumps-advisory-board. Accessed 30 June 2020.

Barlow, Joel. 1796. "Treaty of Peace and Friendship between the United States of America and the Bey and Subjects of Tripoli of Barbary." Internet resource available from https://avalon.law.yale.edu/18th_century/bar1796t.asp. Accessed 4 July 2020.

Barna Group. 2020. "One in Three Practicing Christians Has Stopped Attending Church During COVID-19." Internet resource available from https://www.barna.com/research/new-sunday-morning-part-2/. Accessed 8 July 2020.

Bebbington, David. 1989. *Evangelicalism in Modern Britain: A History from the 1730s to the 1980s*. London: Unwin Hyman.

Beckford, James. 1993. "Are New Religious Movements New Social Movements?" *Scriptura* 12: 19-34.

Bediako, Kwame. 1992. *Theology and Identity: The Impact of Culture upon Christian Thought in the Second Century and Modern Africa*. Carlisle, UK: Regnum Books.

Bhatia, Kathy Richards and Michael T. Cooper. Forthcoming. *Social Injustice: An Evangelical Voice in Tumultuous Times*. Ephesiology Press.

Black Lives Matter Foundation, Inc. Internet resource available from http://blacklivesmatter.org. Accessed 27 July 2020.

Brenan, Megan. 2017. "Nurses Keep Healthy Lead as Most Honest, Ethical Profession." Internet resource available from https://news.gallup.com/poll/224639/nurses-keep-healthy-lead-honest-ethical-profession.aspx. Accessed July 9, 2020.

Carter, Joe. 2015. "Fact Checker: Are all Christian Denominations in Decline?" The Gospel Coalition. Internet resource available from https://www.thegospelcoalition.org/article/factchecker-are-all-christian-denominations-in-decline/. Accessed 26 July 2020.

Cooper, Michael T. 2018. "Not on Our Watch: Five Distraction from Fulfilling the Great Commission," *Evangelical Missions Quarterly* Vol. 54, Issue 2: 8-13.

___________. 2020. *Ephesiology: The Study of the Ephesian Movement*. Littleton, CO: William Carey Publisher.

Cooper, Michael T. and Matt Till. 2020. *Crises and the Church: Lessons from History*. Ephesiology Press.

Denker, Angela. 2020. "Who are the Catholics who voted for Trump," *U.S. Catholic*. Internet resource available from http://www.uscatholic.org/print/31946. Accessed 26 June 2020.

Ephesiology Podcast. 2020. "Interview with Alan Hirsch." Internet resource available from https://ephesiology.com/2020/01/28/ep-35-interview-with-alan-hirsch/.

Evangelical Focus Europe. "660 million evangelicals in the world?" Internet resource available from https://evangelicalfocus.com/world/5119/660-million-evangelicals-in-the-world. Accessed 26 June 2020.

Fahmy, Dalia. 2020. "Most Americans don't see Trump as religious; fewer than half say they think he's Christian." Pew Research Center. Internet resource available from https://www.pewresearch.org/fact-tank/2020/03/25/most-americans-dont-see-trump-as-religious/. Accessed 27 June 2020.

Galli, Mark. 2019. "Trump Should be Removed from Office." *Christianity Today*. Internet resource available from https://www.christianitytoday.com/ct/2019/december-web-only/trump-should-be-removed-from-office.html. Accessed 19 December 2020.

Grudem, Wayne. 2016. "Why Voting for Donald Trump is a Morally Good Choice." Townhall. Internet resource available from https://townhall.com/columnists/waynegrudem/2016/07/28/why-voting-for-donald-trump-is-a-morally-good-choice-n2199564. Accessed 4 July 2020.

Heimoff, Steve. 2020. "Evangelicals, Trump, and COVID-19." Internet resource available from http://www.steveheimoff.com/index.php/2020/04/18/evangelicals-trump-and-covid-19/. Accessed 27 July 2020.

Holcombe, Lee and Ray Kuntz. 2020. "COVID-19: The Effects on Ministry Giving." Internet resource available from https://deo-volente.org/wp-content/uploads/2020/04/COVID-19-The-Effects-on-Ministry-Giving-.pdf. Accessed July 8, 2020.

Johnson, Todd M. and Gina A. Zurlo. 2020. *World Christian Database*. Boston: Brill.

Jones, Robert P. 2019. "White Christian America Ended in the 2010s." Internet resource available from https://www.nbcnews.com/think/opinion/2010s-spelled-end-white-christian-america-ncna1106936. Accessed July 9, 2020.

Kruse, Michael. 2018. "I Need Loyalty." *Politico*. Internet resource available from https://www.politico.com/magazine/story/2018/03/06/donald-trump-loyalty-staff-217227. Accessed 26 June 2020.

LaFrance, Adrienne. 2020. "The Prophecies of Q: American conspiracy theories are entering a dangerous new phase." *The Atlantic*.

https://www.theatlantic.com/magazine/archive/2020/06/qanon-nothing-can-stop-what-is-coming/610567/

McGrath, Alister. 1995. *Evangelicalism and the Future of Christianity*. Downers Grove: Intervaristy Press.

McNeel, Bekah. 2019. "Latinos Immigrants are Evangelizing America." *Christianity Today*. Internet resource available from https://www.christianitytoday.com/news/2019/july/hispanic-church-planting-survey-immigration-evangelism.html. Accessed 27 June 2020.

Metaxas, Eric. "Interview with Franklin Graham." The Eric Metaxas Radio Show. Internet resource available from https://www.metaxastalk.com/podcast/wednesday-november-20-2019/. Accessed 21 November 2019.

Nassif, Bradley. 1998. "New Dimension in Eastern Orthodox Theology." In *New dimensions in Evangelical thought: Essays in honor of Millard J. Erickson*, ed. David S. Dockery, 92-117. Downers Grove: Intervarsity.

Oden, Thomas. 1992. *After Modernity . . . What? Agenda for Theology*. Grand Rapids: Zondervan.

__________. 1996. "Why We Believe in Heresy," *Christianity Today* 40, no. 3: 12-13.

Operation World. N.d. "Evangelical Growth." Internet resource available from http://www.operationworld.org/hidden/evangelical-growth. Access 26 June 2020.

Packard, Joshua and Ashleigh Hope. 2015. *Church Refugees: Sociologists Reveal Why People are DONE with Church but not Their Faith*. Loveland, CO: Group Publishing.

Packard, Joshua. 2015. *Exodus of the Religious Dones: Research Reveals the Size, Make-Up, and Motivations of the Formerly Churched Population*. Loveland, CO: Group Publishing.

Pew Research Center. 2011. "Christian Movements and Denominations." Pew Research Center. Internet resource available from https://www.pewforum.org/2011/12/19/global-christianity-movements-and-denominations/. Accessed 20 June 2020.

___________. 2014. "The Shifting Religious Identity of Latinos in the United States." Pew Research Center. Internet resource available from https://www.pewforum.org/2014/05/07/the-shifting-religious-identity-of-latinos-in-the-united-states/. Accessed 30 June 2020.

___________. 2016. "How the faithful voted: A preliminary 2016 analysis." Pew Research Center. Internet resource available from https://www.pewresearch.org/fact-tank/2016/11/09/how-the-faithful-voted-a-preliminary-2016-analysis/. Accessed 30 June 2020.

Piper, John. 2020. "How Much Patriotism is too Much Patriotism?" *Ask Pastor John Podcast*. Internet resource available from https://www.desiringgod.org/interviews/how-much-patriotism-is-too-much-patriotism. Accessed 3 July 2020.

PRRI Staff. 2020. "Trump Favorability Slips Among White Catholics and Non-College Americans During National Unresest." Public Religion Research Institute. Internet resource available from https://www.prri.org/research/trump-favorability-white-catholic-and-non-college-americans-national-unrest-protests/. Accessed 26 June 2020.

Rainer, Thom S. 2020. "Major New Research on Declining, Plateaued, and Growing Churches from Exponential and Lifeway Research." Internet resource available from https://www.pewresearch.org/fact-tank/2020/01/28/u-s-churchgoers-are-satisfied-with-the-sermons-they-hear-though-content-varies-by-religious-tradition/

Schwadel, Philip and Gregory A. Smith. 2019. "White evangelical Protestants consistently give President Trump high marks."

Pew Research Center. Internet resource available from https://www.pewresearch.org/fact-tank/2019/03/18/evangelical-approval-of-trump-remains-high-but-other-religious-groups-are-less-supportive/. Accessed 30 June 2020.

Steinbuch, Yaron. 2020. "Black Lives Matter co-founder describes herself as 'trained Marxist.'" *New York Post*. Internet resource available from https://nypost.com/2020/06/25/blm-co-founder-describes-herself-as-trained-marxist/. Accessed 5 July 2020.

Teague, Matthew. 2020. "'He wears the armor of God:' evangelicals hail Trump's church photo op." *The Guardian*. Internet resource available from https://www.theguardian.com/us-news/2020/jun/03/donald-trump-church-photo-op-evangelicals. Accessed 3 June 2020.

The Joshua Project. "Global Statistics." Internet resource available from https://joshuaproject.net/people_groups/statistics. Accessed 20 June 2020.

The State of Theology. 2018. "The 2018 State of Theology Survey." Internet resource available from https://thestateoftheology.com. Accessed July 8, 2020.

The Wealth Record. 2020. "Franklin Graham Net Worth." Internet resource available from https://www.thewealthrecord.com/celebs-bio-wiki-salary-earnings-2019-2020-2021-2022-2023-2024-2025/pastor/franklin-graham-net-worth/. Accessed 30 June 2020.

___________. 2020. "Robert Jeffress Net Worth." Internet resource available from https://www.thewealthrecord.com/celebs-bio-wiki-salary-earnings-2019-2020-2021-2022-2023-2024-2025/pastor/robert-jeffress-net-worth/. Accessed 30 June 2020.

___________. 2020. "Jerry Falwell, Jr. Net Worth." Internet resource available from https://www.thewealthrecord.com/celebs-bio-wiki-salary-earnings-2019-2020-2021-2022-2023-2024-2025/lawyer/jerry-falwell-jr-net-worth/. Accessed 30 June 2020.

__________. 2019. "Paula White Net Worth." Internet resource available from https://www.thewealthrecord.com/celebs-bio-wiki-salary-earnings-2019-2020-2021-2022-2023-2024-2025/pastor/paula-white-net-worth/. Accessed 30 June 2020.

US Census Bureau. 2019. "2019 U.S. Population Estimates Continue to Show the Nation's Growth is Slowing." Internet resource available from https://www.census.gov/newsroom/press-releases/2019/popest-nation.html. Accessed 30 June 2020.

Van Rooy, Jacobus, A. 1985. "Christ and the Religions: The Issues at Stake." *Missionalia* 13.1: 3-13.

Wehner, Peter. 2019. "Are Trump's Critics Demonically Possessed?" The Atlantic. Internet resource available from https://www.theatlantic.com/ideas/archive/2019/11/to-trumps-evangelicals-everyone-else-is-a-sinner/602569/. Accessed 1 August 2020.

Whitehead, Andrew L., Samuel L. Perry, and Joseph O. Baker. 2018. "Make America Christian Again: Christian Nationalism and Voting for Donald Trump in the 2016 Presidential Election." *Sociology of Religion* 79, no. 2: 147-71. https://doi.org/10.1093/socrel/srx070.

ANCIENT SOURCES

Appian. *The Civil Wars.*

Augustine. Letter XCIII.

Augustine. *The Literal Meaning of Genesis.*

Irenaeus. *Against Heresies*

Jerome. *Commentary on Matthew.*

Tertullian. *On Idolatry.*

Victorinus, Marius. *Commentary on the Letter to the Ephesians*

ABOUT THE AUTHOR

Michael T. Cooper is missiologist-in-residence at East West Ministries International and the Program Director of the Master of Arts in Missiology of Movements at Mission India Theological Seminary. He earned a PhD in Intercultural Studies with a focus on religious movements and a minor in theology from Trinity Evangelical Divinity School. He currently focuses on missiological research and equipping missionaries for effective cultural engagement. He has thirty years of missions experience, including ten years as a pioneer church planter in Romania after the fall of communism and has equipped church planters and leaders in Africa, Europe, North America, South America, South Asia, and Southeast Asia.

OTHER BOOKS BY MICHAEL

Crises and the Church: Lessons from History. Ephesiology Press, 2020. With Matt Till.

Ephesiology: The Study of a Movement. Littleton: William Carey Publishing, 2020.

Unwrapping the First Christmas. Ephesiology Press, 2019.

God's Mission in the World: A Simple Study of the Bible's Grand Narrative for Oral Learners. Ephesiology Press, 2019.

Editor (with William J. Moulder) and Contributor, *Social Injustice: What Evangelicals Need to Know about the World*. Lake Forest: The Timothy Center Press, 2011.

Editor (with Clifford Williams) and Contributor, *The Peaceable Christian: Five Evangelicals Reflect on Peace*. Lake Forest: The Timothy Center Press, 2011.

Contemporary Druidry: A Historical and Ethnographic Study. Salt Lake City: Sacred Tribes Press, 2010.

Editor and Contributor, *Perspectives on Post—Christendom Spiritualities: Reflections on New Religious Movements and Western Spiritualities*. Sydney, Australia: Morling Press, 2010.

ABOUT EPHESIOLOGY

Ephesiology focuses on the study of the early Christian movement that began in the city of Ephesus. Ephesus was the site of the most significant church-planting movement in the early church, with 40 percent of the New Testament texts relating to it. What made that city the epicenter of the movement? And how can we replicate sustained movements in a world that feels so different? Learn more at https://ephesiology.com

EPHESIOLOGY PODCAST

Join our podcasters each week for a captivating discussion about a New Testament movement that started in Ephesus and impacted all of Asia Minor for 13 centuries. We dig deeply into the missiological theology of the New Testament in order to understand what a movement might look like today.

LOOKING FOR A SPEAKER?

All of our topics can be either in person or via video webinar. Contact us for more information.

Business Luncheon – typically a 30-45 minute talk focused on engaging the business community in the completion of the Great Commission. For audiences of all sizes.

Request Michael

Church Leaders' Luncheon – typically a 30-45 minute talk focused on casting vision for a missiologically theocentric passion for God's glory by joining His mission in pursuit of more worshipers. For audiences of all sizes.

Request Michael, Andrew or Matt

Sermon – typically a 30-45 minute exegetical sermon focused on one of the following topics: launching a movement, grounding a movement, leading a movement, multiplying a movement, or sustaining a movement.

Request Michael, Andrew or Matt

Shepherding Your Church to Movement – one day seminar focused on a missiologically theocentric ecclesiology expressed in four salient features: praxis, koinonia, hermeneutics, leaders. We also design a unique online interactive experience for participants. For audiences of all sizes.

Request Michael or Matt

Movement Workshop – a two day workshop focused on discovering principles of a missiologically theocentric movement that effectively engages a community by connecting Jesus's story to the story of the people. The workshop culminates in a movement action plan uniquely designed to engage your community, disciple new believers, develop leaders, and establish healthy communities of Christ-followers. Includes a free copy of *Ephesiology: The Study of the Ephesian Movement*. Limited to 20 key leaders.

EPHESIOLOGY MASTER CLASSES

An Ephesiology Master Class is not your typical seminary course. In fact, this is learning designed with you in mind. Our classes are especially designed for an online and engaging experience that is focused on your learning goals.

Since we have been where you are, we focus on content that we know will help you succeed in multiplying disciples, planting churches, and crossing cultures.

Focused on those who want the missions and ministry skills without the price tag of a seminary, we have designed a platform that is accessible 24/7 from anywhere in the world and will not put you in debt. The collaborative nature of our classes will enhance the sense of community where innovation and creativity can thrive. This is a learning experience designed with the practitioner in mind.

Discover God's passion for movements

This is not another methodology or attempt to re-contextualize evangelicalism. Rather, it is a journey from the launch of the church in Ephesus as it became a movement grounded in God's mission and led by those who multiplied generations of Christ-followers. The *Ephesiology Movement Workshop* focuses on you and your team as missiological theologians who successfully connect Jesus's story with the cultural context and narrative of the people in your community. You'll discover how to relate the God of all creation to a people who seek him in vain and how effective engagement can result in transforming the religious, intellectual, economic, and social fabrics of a community.

The *Ephesiology Movement Workshop* offers a comprehensive view of the redemptive movement of the Holy Spirit in Ephesus and compels us to ask the question: How can we effectively connect Christ to our culture? Through interacting with the Ephesian movement, you'll discover how the Holy-Spirit still changes lives, cities, and the world.

WHAT TO EXPECT

Ephesiology Movement Workshop participants discover how to:

1. Effectively speak about God's mission in the world and the church's role in it.
2. Use biblical principles of dialogue, observation, and historical study to identify their community's story.
3. Connect God's story to the community's story.
4. Develop a plan of action to uniquely communicate God's story and make more disciples of Jesus Christ.
5. Participate in God's mission of more people worshiping Him in their community and around the world.
6. Lead a church and leadership board in developing a Movement Action Plan focused on the engagement of their community.

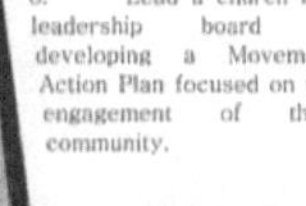

Free book for all participants

ABOUT THE FACILITATOR

MICHAEL T. COOPER currently serves as an executive for a missions agency, training national leaders in evangelism, discipleship, leadership development, and church planting. He is the former president and CEO of an international NGO. In 2010, he founded a Business as Mission initiative that focused on helping alleviate spiritual and economic poverty in the developing world. For a decade he equipped undergraduate and graduate students at Trinity International University with skills to engage culture. He has thirty years of ministry and missions experience, ten years as a pioneer church planter in Romania after the fall of communism. He holds a MA in Missions from Columbia International University and a PhD in Intercultural Studies from Trinity Evangelical Divinity School. Throughout his career, Michael has focused on creative ways to engage difficult-to-reach people with the gospel.

CONTACT INFORMATION

Email: info@ephesiology.com

Web Page: ephesiology.com

Facebook: @ephesiology

Instagram: ephesiology

ITS TIME FOR A MOVMENT

By focusing on discovery learning, the workshop will have a lasting impact on participants as they uncover biblical principles through the story of the church in Ephesus and apply them in their plan to mature disciples and multiple followers of Christ in their community.

Discover God's passion for movements